The COMPLETELY AMAZING Slightly Outrageous State QUARTERS Atlas and ALBUM

by the editors of Klutz

KLUTZ

KLUTZ ®

is a kids' company staffed entirely by real human beings. We began our corporate life in 1977 in an office we shared with a Chevrolet Impala. Today we've outgrown our founding garage, but Palo Alto, California, remains Klutz galactic headquarters. For those of you who collect corporate mission statements, here's ours:

• Create wonderful things.
• Be good.
• Have fun.

Write Us

We would love to hear your comments regarding this or any of our books. We have many!

Visit Us: 👉 **klutz.com**

KLUTZ

455 Portage Avenue
Palo Alto, CA 94306

Book printed in Korea.
Plastic trays manufactured in Korea.
©2001 Klutz Inc.
All rights reserved.
Klutz® is a registered trademark of Klutz, Inc.
ISBN 1-57054-607-X

4 1 5 8 5 7 0 8 8 8

Do You Teach?

We offer a classroom set of make-your-own Klutz books. E-mail: bookfactory@klutz.com, write, or visit our website for details.

Additional Copies

For the location of your nearest Klutz retailer, call (650) 857-0888. Should they be tragically out of stock, additional copies of this book, and the entire library of 100% Klutz certified books, are available in our mail order catalog. See back page.

Klutz is a Nelvana company

CONTENTS

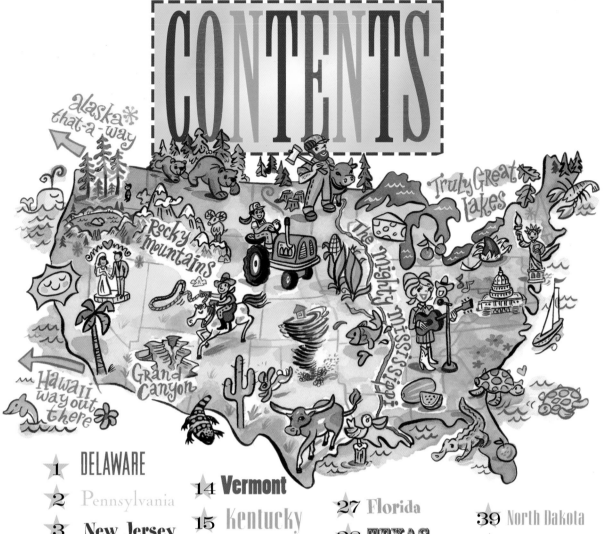

The choice of city was very deliberate since the new design honored Delaware, the very first state to ratify the United States Constitution (back when it was brand new in 1787). The Delaware quarter was the first of 50 new quarters that the mint will be releasing every 10 weeks up until 2008. Each of them will honor a different state and **each design will be produced and released only once.**

The quarters are not going into continuous production; each state will

come out during its 10-week release window, then production will stop and the mint will go on to the next. This "one-and-done" production schedule has turned state quarter collecting into a national frenzy. It's one of the biggest collecting crazes in modern American history.

On **January 1, 1999,** the United States mint released **a newly designed quarter** in the **capital city of the state of Delaware.**

Why Are There Slots for 100 Quarters in this Book, and not 50?

The quarters are produced in two cities, Philadelphia and Denver. A small "P" or "D" under the words "IN GOD WE TRUST" indicates where the coin was minted. A complete collection of the new state quarters would have in it 100 coins — 50 states, two mint marks each. That's why this album has 100 slots — not 50.

The states will be released in the order in which they entered The Union. Five new coins every year. Delaware was the first; Hawaii will be the last. Everybody else comes in-between. The release years are printed in the back of this book on the album pages.

Proof Sets

The mint will also be producing "proof sets" of the quarters that are not intended to circulate and are designed strictly for collectors. The San Francisco mint will be producing those and they will be sold through dealers or the mint itself (check out their website for details or call them at 202-283-2646).

Remember: During the 10 years up to 2008, the "old" quarters, the eagle quarters, will not be made.

How to Fill Out Your Collection

During the 10-week release window, and for a few months afterwards, it should be fairly simple to pick up the new coin in pocket change. If you're on one coast or the other, finding the distant mint mark takes a little luck, but you'll find friends or relatives who live far away are often good for a mailed quarter or two.

As each new state gets less and less new, you'll see its coin start to dry up. The mint is producing nearly a billion of each design, but collectors are taking them out of circulation in staggering numbers. (Nevermind all the coins that roll down the sewer.) To deal with the problem **we suggest patience and snooping.** Ask for your change in quarters. Find friendly grocery store clerks. Ask your parents to keep an eye out. Look under the sofa cushions and back seat. They're still out there.

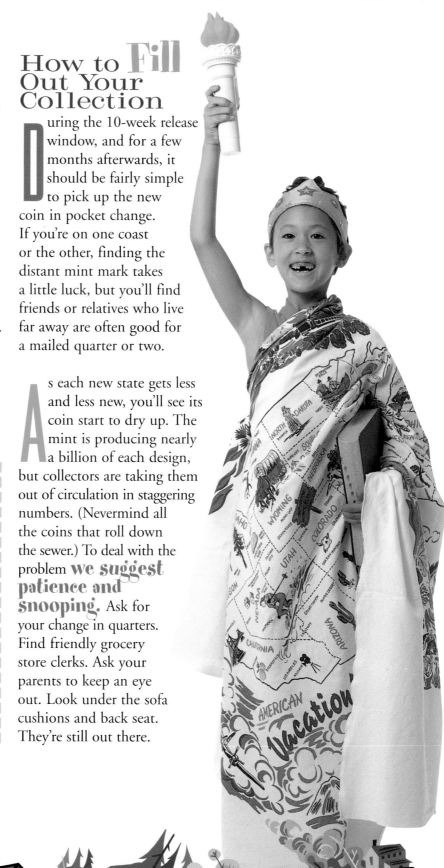

What **If I Want** to **Design** a New Quarter Myself?
Great idea!

Each state gets to choose its own design, although the federal government has to give final approval. Typically, the governor issues a call to a select group of artists who live in the state to submit designs, but "open calls" also exist in which anyone who lives in the state — young or old — can submit. If your state is still more than 2 years away from its release, check out your state government's website to see if designs are being sought from the public.

Fair warning: It won't work to submit a picture of yourself. The mint says "no living people."

DELAWARE

Our Favorite

Annie Jump Cannon

(1863–1941) A real star. Astronomer who developed the system of classification of stars by their spectra. The system groups stars into categories labeled O, B, A, F, G, K, and M (known by the mnemonic, "Oh, Be A Fine Girl, Kiss Me").

Delaware is only 35 miles wide at its widest point. The narrowest part of the state is just 8 miles wide; you can walk it in a day. Its northern border forms the arc of a perfect circle.

You've Probably Eaten a Delawarean.

*The most popular zip code for chickens in the country is 19970, ① **Sussex County.** Most of them are short-term residents, though (9–12 weeks).*

Shortest part of the state is 8 miles, nothing but a nice morning's walk

*It Started with a Bang. In 1802, French immigrant Eleuthére Irénée du Pont built a small gunpowder factory near ② **Wilmington,** DE. It was the start of the multi-billion-dollar DuPont Chemical Co., which, together with the DuPont family, have been major factors throughout Delaware's history. You can experience a bit of DuPont yourself just by finding a plastic bottle of soda pop (with 23 billion of them made every year, it's not hard). The first PET bottle was patented by DuPont in 1973. (Nylon, another DuPont invention, came in 1934.)*

③ **Newark** *Let it rain. Gore-Tex was invented here. The material was originally used as a waterproof casing for electrical wires.*

④ **Dover** *The Victor Talking Machine Company started here in 1901. There's a Victrola Museum in town — precursor to today's boombox. It's also home to Dover Air Force Base.*

Widest part of the state is 35 miles

Ever Seen a 400-mph pumpkin?

Check out the annual Punkin' Chunkin Festival in ⑤ Lewes. Teams from around the country compete to build catapults capable of launching pumpkins much farther than leading scientists used to believe was possible. Pumpkins must leave the device "intact" and no explosives of any kind allowed (darn). 1999 record? 3,694 feet. (Get WAY back. That's three-fourths of a mile.)

So THAT'S where Mudville is. ⑥ **Millsboro** *is where Major League Baseball gets some of its ball-rubbing mud every summer.*

Beach Blankets and Bureaucrats.
Washington, D.C., gets its tan at ⑦ **Rehoboth Beach** every summer, when the town's population explodes. First U.S. beauty contest held here in 1880 (Thomas Edison was there to help judge).

Most Famous

Caesar Rodney

(1728–1784) When the new Continental Congress prepared to vote on the fateful break with England in July of 1776, Caesar Rodney, one of the Delaware representatives, rode a stormy 80 miles to Philadelphia to break a tie in his state's 3-man delegation. Along with fellow representative Thomas McKean, he put Delaware on the side of independence. Caesar's heroic ride is commemorated on the state's quarter.

THOMAS McKEAN SENDS A LETTER TO CAESAR RODNEY.

DEAR CAESAR, YOU MUST COME VOTE TO SETTLE THE QUESTION OF INDEPENDENCE.

RODNEY RODE ON DESPITE THE TORMENT OF HIS ILLNESS AND THE TORTURE OF THE WEATHER!

I VOTE FOR INDEPENDENCE!

{PENNSYLVANIA}

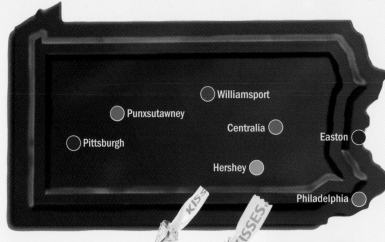

MOST FAMOUS
Rachel Carson

(1907–1964) Marine biologist whose book *Silent Spring* is often credited with starting the modern environmental movement. Many pesticides, including DDT, were banned or brought under control because of her book.

Here's a few of our favorite Pennsylvania things: **Crayola Crayons, Wooly Willy and Slinky**

(invented by an engineer who was messing around with springs when one fell off a shelf – and started walking away), Stetson cowboy hats (1865), Hires Root Beer (1875) and Martin guitars (1833).

OUR FAVORITE
Philip Morrison

Scientist Phillip Morrison (b. 1915) is the owner of one of the larger brains in North America and, even rarer, a man who appears to be genetically incapable of boredom — nothing fails to interest him. Although the list of his books, articles and publications is staggering, it omits the big book that he and Phylis Morrison, his wife and co-conspirator, have written with their distinguished lives. We'd call it The Joy of Science, or, perhaps more accurately, The Joy of Life.

Philadelphia

is the nation's leader in weird museums. It's where you can find things like the Museum of Mourning Art, the Insectarium, the Garbage Disposal Museum and the granddaddy of all weird museums, the Mütter Museum, home of President Grover Cleveland's jaw tumor (in a jar) and a fascinating collection of 2,000 things doctors have removed from people's stomachs.

And while we're in this area, we will note that the first toilet paper company to experience the flush of commercial success was the Scott Paper Company, Philadelphia, PA.

The **first** *Girl Scout cookie ever sold, was sold in Philadelphia (1934).*

Monopoly

Charles B. Darrow, a Philadelphian, invented the game by sketching on his tablecloth (1934).

Hershey

is home of the Hershey Candy Company, where a guy can receive 32 million kisses a day. The company was started by Milton Hershey who gave half of the company's stock to a school for orphaned boys (they still own it). Good amusement park in town.

Pittsburgh

is, first and foremost, the neighborhood of Mr. Rogers, the most respectable man on television. (Our favorite show is the one where he goes to the Crayola factory in Easton, Pennsylvania, and personally makes the one-billionth crayon.)

Centralia

is home to the most infamous coal mine fire in America, burning under the town since 1962 with no end in sight. The state bought up most of its houses and Centralia is now little more than a ghost town with smoke coming up out of the cracks and ground that can be warm to the touch.

Ben Franklin,

who lived most of his life in Philadelphia, is the owner of one of our favorite brains. A very partial list of his accomplishments: bifocals, wood stoves, rocking chairs, lightning rods, public libraries and, of course, he had a major hand in the writing of both the Declaration of Independence and the Constitution. (He was a publisher of a popular book, too. We always like that.)

Williamsport

is where Carl Stotz founded Little League in 1939. (He left disgusted in 1955, saying the League had lost track of who the game was for.) The Little League World Series is held here every year.

Punxsutawney Phil

Each year on February 2nd Punxsutawney Phil predicts the weather. If he sees his shadow, folks can expect six more weeks of winter.

New Jersey

1 Menlo Park, NJ, workplace of America's most famous inventor, Thomas Edison (the Bill Gates of his era). Edison basically lived at his lab, sleeping only in catnaps while he invented things like the electric light bulb.

2 In 1938, a famous radio show was broadcast with a fake news flash and follow-up story about an enormous alien attack. The show was taken seriously and mass hysteria ensued all over the northeast. According to the show, the aliens landed in the little town of Grover's Mills, NJ.

3 The Ah-Choo Sneezing Powder Co. (now called the S.S. Adams Co.) is located here in Neptune, NJ. It is the largest supplier of handshake buzzers, disappearing ink, whoopie cushions and sneezing powder in the U.S. today.

4 Albert Einstein, Time Magazine's "Man of the 20th Century," lived at 112 Mercer Street, Princeton, NJ. The house is still there.

5 Mmmm mmmm good. **The Campbell Soup Company** is located here. Cans, incidentally, were invented before can openers. Early cans came with the instructions: Open with chisel and hammer.

6 **Wildwood-by-the-Sea,** NJ. Home of the National Marbles Championships (held every summer).

7 **The New Jersey Devil,** a very shy ape-like animal, lives in the New Jersey Pine Barrens, a densely wooded section of the state. A lot of the people who have seen the Devil have seen UFOs too.

★ **Trenton,** where George Washington crossed the Delaware, Christmas night, 1776.

Most Famous

Jack Nicholson (b.1937) One of Hollywood's greatest actors takes over any scene he's in. If the Lakers are in the play-offs, his brain turns into a basketball.

Our Favorite

Paul Robeson (1898–1976) An African American man who lived a huge life. Singer, actor, human rights activist, lawyer and athlete. He towered in every field.

GEORGIA

Atlanta

The most widely recognized symbol on the planet is Coca-Cola owned by the Coca-Cola Company headquartered in Atlanta. 1 *The drink was invented by John Pemberton, an Atlanta drugstore owner in 1886. It was sold after his death for* **$2300**. *The* **original Coke was green** *and contained traces of cocaine. That is no longer the case. All the Coca-Cola that the world drinks in a single day would run Niagara Falls for 28 seconds.*

Brer Rabbit

is from Georgia (so is his briar patch and creator, Joel Chandler Harris*).*

Cleveland

Birthplace of Cabbage Patch Dolls, 1978. 8 **(In 1985, at the peak of the fad, Christmas shortages created store riots.)**

Sweet Vidalia onions 9 *are from Georgia.*

Oliver Hardy

(1892–1957) Along with Stan Laurel, made up one-half of the funniest comedy team in Hollywood's history. Proof? Rent *Sons of the Desert*.

Paradise Gardens

Crazed carpenter **Howard Finster** *has built and painted an eccentric* **"art house"** *here that defies description, convention and gravity.*

Dr. Martin Luther King, Jr.
(1929–1968) His church, the Ebenezer Baptist, 2 is in Atlanta where he is buried. His leadership of the Civil Rights movement has made him the most widely acclaimed African American leader in United States history.

Stone Mountain

The world's largest sculpture, depicting Confederate heroes Stonewall Jackson, Jefferson Davis and Robert E. Lee.

Margaret Mitchell

wrote **Gone with the Wind** *in Georgia in 1936. Immortal last line? "...Tomorrow is another day."*

More sights in Georgia include **Lookout Mountain** 3 *(see 7 states from the top on a clear day),* **Okefenokee Swamp** 4 *(famous for ferocious alligators),* **Dahlonega** 5 *(site of America's first major gold rush; you can still find gold here), and* **Savannah** 6 *(site of the first Girl Scout Troop in the U.S., 1912).*

Gullah

An African-flavored dialect of English still spoken on the 10 Sea Islands 7 *off the coast of Georgia.*

Former President **Jimmy Carter** *is from Plains, GA,* 10 *which, incidentally, is good* **peanut** *growing country (not bad for* **pecans** *and* **peaches** *either).*

If yo' play wild puppy ee lick yo' face.*

*(Translation? Familiarity breeds contempt.)

Connecticut

Enfield

Hartford

Orange
is where you can find corporate headquarters for Pez Candies, one of the few candy companies where the candy isn't really the story; it's the dispensers.

Rocky Hill
Dinosaurs left a good set of footprints here roughly 100 million years ago.

You can see a stately tree, **The Charter Oak,** pictured on the back of the Connecticut quarter. Legend has it that in 1687 the state's all-important charter (its "birth certificate") was hidden in this tree when British officers demanded its surrender.

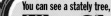

The squeezable toothpaste tube was developed in New Haven in 1892.

Silly Putty was a by-product of WWII research in Stamford.

Old Lyme
Bring one along and get into the Nut Museum for free.

Most Famous

Stamford
Although a great many global corporations are headquartered in Connecticut, we have a few favorites: The World Wrestling Federation operates out of Stamford and we don't know about you but we were shocked (SHOCKED!) to recently learn, from congressional testimony, that WWF matches are NOT real sport! They're "entertainment."

Bridgeport
is home to the Barnum Circus Museum. P.T. ("There's a sucker born every minute") Barnum was the founder of "The Greatest Show on Earth."

Enfield,
just across the way from the state penitentiary, is U.S. headquarters for the Danish company LEGO Systems. The next time you step on one of those little bricks in your bare feet, just remember, the chances are excellent it's from Connecticut.

New Haven

Yale University is in New Haven, the home of the Frisbie Pie Baking Co. According to legend, Yalies would polish off a Frisbie pie and then let fly with the tin. The name (and habit) came to the attention of the Wham-O Corp. (Calif.), makers of a brand new toy they were calling the "Pluto Platter." The Wham-O guys knew a better name when they heard it and the "Pluto Platter" was (thankfully) rechristened.

Our Favorite

Katharine Hepburn
(b. 1909) One of America's most beloved actors, a classy mix of looks, brains and style. Rent anything with her and Bogart or Spencer Tracy.

Nathan Hale
A Revolutionary War hero who volunteered for spy duty behind enemy lines. He was caught and summarily hung. Last words? *"I only regret that I have but one life to give for my country."*

State fish:

sperm whale (Yes, you should write and tell them.)

5

Massachusetts

Yes, *Massachusetts is the cradle of American independence, and Massachusetts is where that famous bit of patriotic vandalism, the* **Boston Tea Party,** *took place.* ❶ Lexington, MA, is where patriot Paul Revere took his famous ride, *and the first shots of the American Revolution, "the shots heard round the world," were first heard in Massachusetts. But Massachusetts is bigger than all that. Much bigger. Consider: Massachusetts is the* birthplace *of the plastic pink lawn* flamingo *(❷ Leominster, 1951). It's also the home of* Paul Tavilla; *you can read about him in the Guinness Book of World Records. Paul once caught a grape that had been thrown 396 feet. In his mouth. Also, Massachusetts has the lake with the longest name in the country —* Lake Chaubunagungamaug. ❸

John F. Kennedy
(1917-1963)
35th president of the United States. Kennedy was the youngest man ever elected president and the youngest to die in office. Quote: "Ask not what your country can do for you — ask what you can do for your country."

Massachusetts Bay

Boston

Basketball was invented
in Massachusetts; so was volleyball and the circular saw (by a nun). **Moby Dick** *was written in Massachusetts; so was "Mary Had a Little Lamb" (1817).*

The Basketball Hall of Fame is in ❹ **Springfield, MA, where the biggest attraction is** Bob Lanier's size 22 basketball shoes.

The capital of Massachusetts is ⭐ *Boston where the expression* **"OK"** *was first used (it was supposed to be funny for "oll korrect" in 1830). Boston is home to* **Curious George** *and* **Peter Cottontail.** *Plus it's the place where baked beans were first consumed.* ❺ *Cambridge, MA, is where you can find over forty* Nobel Prize–winners, Harvard University, the Massachusetts Institute of Technology and the Necco Co., *where nearly all of the country's* **"valentine conversation hearts"** *are made. Chocolate chip cookies were invented in Whitman (1930).*

Dr. Seuss
(a.k.a. Theodor Seuss Geisel, 1904-1991)
Hard to believe that in only one brain you could fit the house on Mulberry Street, Horton, his egg, Bartholomew and his hats, all those Who's, a Grinch, Yertle, green eggs and ham, the Lorax, plus of course, that cat and his hat.

OUR FAVORITE

Emily Dickinson,
famous poet, lived all her life in a house in ❻ *Amherst, MA, where she published only one poem (and wrote thousands).*

Harvey Ball *is another Massachusettan. Harvey designed the yellow smiley smile (1963, for $450).*

Maryland

The Chesapeake Bay Retriever

was developed along the Chesapeake Bay to hunt waterfowl under the worst weather and water conditions. Luckily, the breed generally has a happy disposition.

The Chesapeake Bay is North America's largest estuary (area where fresh and salt water mix) and the world's second largest.

In 1791, *George Washington selected ten square miles of swampland for the creation of a "District of Columbia," the new capital-to-be of the new nation. The location was a compromise.* **It wasn't Boston. It wasn't Richmond.** *It was a new city, with* **no baggage** *or ties to New England or the Old South.* ★ *The* Star Spangled Banner *has a Maryland birthright. It was written by Francis Scott Key, a Georgetown lawyer who watched the British unsuccessfully bombard Baltimore's Ft. McHenry in 1814. Ironically, the melody is actually an English drinking song, and the original words* are even harder to sing than Key's version.

Camp David. Along with its wars, a great deal of peace has been fomented in Maryland as well. For 50 years, American presidents have been sneaking off to this secluded compound for weekends and conferences. The Camp David Accords, a Middle East peace pact brokered by President Carter, was negotiated here in the woods of northern Maryland.

Camp David

Antietam

Baltimore

Burkittsville

Washington D.C.

Annapolis

CHESAPEAKE BAY

Our Favorite

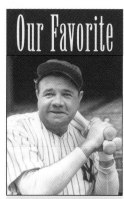

George Herman "Babe" Ruth
(1895—1948)
Yankee Stadium may be the "House That Ruth Built" but you could just as well argue that baseball is the sport that Ruth built. As a kid in Baltimore, Ruth was probably headed for trouble when he was shipped off to board at a boys' school. He started in the big leagues as a pitcher with Boston. Four years later, in a move that we personally think was ill-considered, Harry Frazee, the team's owner, sold him to the Yankees for $100,000.

Just off the coast of Maryland, in 95 feet of water, lies the German submarine U-1105, the Black Panther. *It was scuttled by the U.S. Navy just after World War II and is now a popular diver's destination.*

Blair Township is NOT in Maryland. And the Blair witch does NOT live there.

This is the official word from the townsfolk of Burkittsville, MD, where the Blair Witch Project was filmed and where the locals are now thoroughly sick of filmstruck strangers rummaging through their entirely witchless woods.

The Herndon Monument is a 50-foot cement tower located at the U.S. Naval Academy in Annapolis, MD. It's a challenging climb, particularly when **it is coated with grease** as it is once a year by thoughtful upperclassmen at the Academy. They do it for the benefit of the plebes (first-year students) who then have to climb it in order to move onward and upward to more exalted second-year status.

In reward for their generosity in hosting the nation's capital, Maryland has had more than its share of bloodshed. **In 1814,** *a British invading force landed in Maryland and marched straightaway to the new capital and the White House, which they promptly burned.*

During the Civil War,

Washington was again the focus of an attack and again Maryland was the battleground. The worst came on September 17, 1862, during the battle of Antietam (battlefield shown above), "the bloodiest day in American history."

7

South Carolina

1

The only BMW plant in the U.S. is in Greer. It's the **birthplace of James Bond's Z3 roadster** — the one he drives in "Golden Eye."

Most Famous
Francis Marion, a.k.a. The Swamp Fox (1732?–1795)
American soldier during the Revolutionary War (1775–1783). The British gave him the nickname because he was good at hiding in swamps.

2

Salley, **the Chitlin' Capital of the World,** *hosts an annual Chitlin' Strut (parade). The chitlin' strut is also a dance that's hard to describe, but easy to imagine. Chitlins are hog intestines and, from what we've heard, it's best to get someone else to clean them.*

3

Happy Thanksgiving — Edgefield is home to the **National Wild Turkey Federation.**

4

Pocotaligo *was named by the Yemassee Indians and means "gathering place." We mention this because many folks think the town name originated when someone advised the owner of a lazy town mule to "Poke 'e tail and 'e go." Lesson: It pays to do your research.*

5

Top off the chitlins with a bowl of grits in **St. George;** *they host the* **World Grits Festival.**

6

In **Bluffton** stands a church built in 1753, burned by the British in 1779, rebuilt, and burned again by Sherman in 1865. It's now in ruins, but still has Civil War era graffiti on the walls. Spooky place.

7

St. Helena Island, *one of the Sea Islands, is the location of Penn Center, the first school for freed slaves. The Sea Islands are also home to the Gullah culture, which has its own language. Seagrass baskets are beautifully made here.*

8

The Charleston *dance is thought to have originated with African Americans living on a small island near Charleston, SC. The town is also famous as the location of the first shot of the Civil War (fired at Fort Sumter on April 21, 1861).*

9

Loggerhead turtles live on **Hilton Head Island** *and along the South Carolina coast. Females return to the same beach where they hatched to nest.*

Columbia is the state capital. The state bird, which appears on the South Carolina state quarter, is the Carolina wren, a "friendly and companionable bird which sings practically the year round." Also on the quarter, see why the state is called "The Palmetto State." (Hint: It's a tree.)

10

Mars Bluff *is one of the few cities in the world to have survived a nuclear bomb drop. A U.S. military jet accidently dropped one here in 1958. It fell in a vegetable garden and slightly damaged a church and five houses. Whoops! "Sorry about those tomatoes, ma'am."*

Our Favorite
Dizzy Gillespie, a.ka. John Birks Gillespie (1917–1993)
Famous for puffy cheeks and great jazz trumpet playing, he was called Dizzy because he liked to clown around on stage.

NEW HAMPSHIRE

Sarah Josepha Hale

(1788–1879) The New Hampshire woman who gave us "Mary Had a Little Lamb" is the same woman who convinced Abraham Lincoln to declare Thanksgving a national holiday.

Of all the states in the Union,

New Hampshire may be the most stable. You can start with its geology **(solid granite)** *but its citizens are similarly permanent. While the rest of the U.S. has grown 60-fold since the Revolution, New Hampshire has only grown a tenth of that. There's a no-nonsense grown-up feeling in New Hampshire. If all the states were graduating from high school, we think New Hampshire would be voted "Most Likely to Get Married and Have a Family First."*

Old Man of the Mountain

The most famous face in New Hampshire belongs to a mountain at Franconia Notch. It's been a landmark since Daniel Webster's time, although these days the Old Man has had to get a nose job (steel cables) to keep him looking all together.

The top of **Mount Washington** *has a serious claim for the title "Place with the Worst Weather in the Country." Winds on Mt. Washington are routinely over 100 mph and the gust record is a breezy 231 mph (bodies will fly away at that speed). Mt. Washington is in the White Mountains, incidentally, a chain that is half in Scotland and half here. It dates from the days when Europe and the U.S. were connected.*

SUGAR HILL

MOUNT WASHINGTON

OLD MAN OF THE MOUNTAIN

NORTH CONWAY

Sugar Hill The state sport of New Hampshire is skiing. The country's first ski school was established here in 1927.

CONCORD ☆

KEENE

EAST DERRY

The New Hampshire license plate contains the state motto: **"Live Free or Die."** *The plates are made by inmates at the state penitentiary.*

Uncle Sam

The story goes like this: In 1812, Samuel Wilson, a supplier for the U.S. Army from Mason, New Hampshire, labelled his army-bound goods "U.S." For the soldiers in New Hampshire, the letters "U.S." on the box meant it must have come from old Uncle Sam Wilson. (Amazing how little things can get out of hand...)

New Hampshire Gets Goofy

Forget what we said about state maturity. Here's the REAL New Hampshire.

Alan Shepard

from East Derry, NH, is justly famous as America's First Man in Space. But what is not so well known is that he is also America's **First Golfer on the Moon.** *On January 31, 1971, using a smuggled-on golf club, Shepard hit a golf ball "miles and miles and miles" while standing on the surface of the moon.*

The Mud Bowl

Championships are held every year at the Hog Coliseum (North Conway, NH) which is, perhaps, the only dedicated arena for Mud Football in the world today. They have teams, a league, championships, everything except rules. If you're lucky, you can catch a performance of the New Hampshire Lawn Chair Precision Drill Team during one of the half times.

Sure, a lot of American towns have pumpkin festivals every October, but the Big One – the Pumpkin Super Bowl – is in Keene, NH.

VIRGINIA

Ella Fitzgerald

(1917–1996) *The First Lady of Song. Probably the most admired and recognized female singer of the 20th century.*

Battlefield

More than half of the major battles of the Civil War took place in Virginia where more American soldiers have died than on the soil of any foreign country.

Pocahontas,

the daughter of a local chieftan, married John Rolfe, one of Jamestown's founders and apparently the first white man to grow tobacco ("the precious stink" as one early settler described it). Virginia was founded on tobacco and it remains their largest money crop.

Colonial Williamsburg

You can see what it was like to live in the 18th century at the country's largest outdoor history museum. Real people in the roles of 18th century characters are there to talk to, and you can play roles yourself in the militia and fire brigade.

Suffolk

Home of Mr. Peanut. He was designed in 1906 by a 13-year-old, Antonio Gentile, who won $5 for his idea. The first peanuts in America were planted in Virginia.

Williamsburg
Roanoke
Richmond
Jamestown

Roanoke

Home (maybe) to the most sought-after buried treasure on American soil. According to the story, a man named Thomas Beale buried a huge treasure somewhere near Roanoke, VA, in 1822, leaving a coded description of the location, only portions of which have ever been figured out. The treasure is still out there and many are still in the hunt. Stay tuned…

Chincoteague

A small Virginia island where wild ponies have roamed for hundreds of years (read all about it in "Misty of Chincoteague," a great kids' book). It's also a great shipwreck island. Many of the island's residents are descendants of a shipwrecked boy washed ashore in 1802.

George Washington

(1732–1799) *The commander in chief during the American Revolution and first president of the United States was by all accounts a really good guy. He did not, however, have wooden teeth, chop down a cherry tree, or throw a silver dollar across the Potomac River.*

Pentagon

The U.S. military is head-quartered in Virginia in the Pentagon, the largest office building in the world (17 miles of hall-ways and 68,000 miles of telephone line). Whenever a military crisis develops anywhere in the world, it's monitored here (and in McLean, VA, where the C.I.A. is located).

Jamestown

In 1607, Jamestown, VA, became the first perma-nent English settlement in North America. Since most of the original settlers were "gentlemen" unpre-pared for wilderness living, they died of starvation within a year or two.

Other Favorite Virginians: Richard Byrd *(America's foremost polar explorer. In 1929, 18 years after they were invented, he flew an airplane over the South Pole. Gutsy.)* Arthur Ashe *(The first African American to reach the top of the professional tennis tour. He was class and talent in equal measures.)* Hiram Bingham *(Adventurer-archeologist who makes Indiana Jones look like a 40-pound wimp.)* Grace Hooper *(Computer pioneer and inventor of COBOL programming language, she was also one of the most admired senior officers in the U.S. Navy.)* Wilmer McLean *(The man who saw the start and finish of the Civil War. One of the first artillery shells fired in the first battle, Bull Run, went down his chimney. Seeking peace and quiet, he moved to Appomattox, VA. Four years later, the documents ending the war were signed in his parlor there.)* Meriwether Lewis and James Clark *(Co-captains of the greatest exploration in American history.)* Thomas Jefferson *(Author of the Declaration of Independence, third President of the U.S., scientist, thinker, archi-tect, writer and, incidentally, a darned good real estate man.)* Secretariat. *(The fastest horse that ever lived was a Virginian.)*

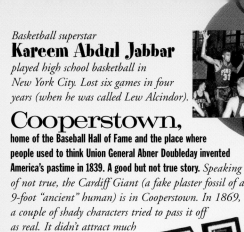

Basketball superstar
Kareem Abdul Jabbar
played high school basketball in New York City. Lost six games in four years (when he was called Lew Alcindor).

Cooperstown,

home of the Baseball Hall of Fame and the place where people used to think Union General Abner Doubleday invented America's pastime in 1839. A good but not true story. *Speaking of not true, the Cardiff Giant (a fake plaster fossil of a 9-foot "ancient" human) is in Cooperstown. In 1869, a couple of shady characters tried to pass it off as real. It didn't attract much notice until it was exposed as a fraud. Then circus legend P.T. Barnum got a hold of it and made a killing by calling it "the greatest hoax in American history."*

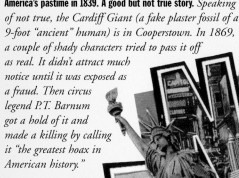

Niagara Falls

October 24, 1901. Retired schoolteacher Annie Taylor (age 63) became the first to go over Niagara Falls in a barrel. Unlike most of the people who've tried it since, she survived. She did it in order to go on a lecture tour about the experience.

SARATOGA SPRINGS •
• NIAGARA FALLS
ALBANY •
• COOPERSTOWN
• ITHACA
NEW YORK CITY •

most famous

**Eleanor Roosevelt (1884–1962)
Franklin D. Roosevelt (1882–1945)**
32nd first lady and president of the United States. Most historians rank FDR as one of the greatest presidents of the 20th century. His wife, Eleanor, gets a similar ranking among first ladies.

our favorite

The Marx Brothers

Chico (1887–1961), Groucho (1890–1977), Harpo (1888–1964), Zeppo (1901–1979) Having a bad day? Rent Night at the Opera *and if that doesn't cure you, you're in deep trouble.*

Statue of Liberty
The index finger of the Statue of Liberty is 8 feet long. The entire statue was made in France.

Essential New York City Facts:

There is a restaurant in New York that serves nothing but peanut butter sandwiches in over 20 varieties. *A guy once jumped off the top of the Empire State Building. He woke up two hours later on a ledge two stories down (windy day). He decided not to commit suicide after all.* **(Going the other way, a footrace is held to the top once a year. Current record? 9 minutes, 53 seconds.)** *"Take Me Out to the Ballgame" was written in 1908 by two guys in New York who'd never seen a ballgame in their lives.* **Frenchman Petit Phillipe once sneaked a cable to the top of one of the World** Trade Center buildings and shot it over to the top of the other one (the old bow and arrow trick). He then proceeded to walk between them — **1,362 ft off the ground. Highly illegal.** *The entire island of*

MANHATTAN

was bought from Native Americans in 1626 by Dutchman Peter Minuit for a legendary $26 in beads. Three hundred and fifty years later, New York City nearly went bankrupt. The Native Americans, in contrast, would have been worth $56,322,268.61 if they had invested their $26 conservatively.

North of New York City, on the way to Ithaca, *the military keeps a number of albino, glow-in-the-dark deer that you can see from the road. No explanation for why.*

Potato chips
George Crum, a Native American cook at a Saratoga Springs resort, one night in 1853 made fried potatoes too thin and crisp to skewer with a fork, but diners loved them then and continue to today.

Dolley Madison (1768–1849)

President James Madison's wife and the only first lady forced to leave the White House in a rush. It was burning at the time, though, set on fire by the British in the War of 1812. Dolley managed to save many of its treasures.

North Carolina

is the kind of state where they have both a Whistling Convention (Louisburg) and a Hollering Convention (Spivey's Corner).

Cape Hatteras Lighthouse

The hazardous waters off Cape Hatteras and Cape Fear are often called the "Graveyard of the Atlantic" because of all the wrecks. Lighthouses have been here since 1803.

High Point

A great town for pulling up a chair and just sitting down (it's the heart of the country's furniture industry).

North Carolina

Boone

Firefly Capital of America.

Kitty Hawk

A pair of bicycle mechanics, Wilbur and Orville Wright, successfully flew in their homemade motor-powered airplane for 12 seconds on December 7, 1903, at Kitty Hawk. Who went first? Orville. (He lost the toss.)

Fayetteville

Birthplace of miniature golf (1954).

Stanfield

The first documented discovery of gold in the country. A 12-year-old kid found a 17-pound gold nugget.

Asheville

You could have the whole town over for a slumber party at America's largest private residence, the Biltmore Estate. It has 250 rooms.

Cherokee

The famed Cherokee Indian Se-quo-yah devised a written form for his language beginning in 1809.

Burlington

Half the socks in the country come from the mills around Burlington. Check out your own. It's probably the left one that's a North Carolinian.

Richard Petty (b. 1937)

"King" Richard, the greatest earning stock car racer ever. Born in a state where they take their stock car racing very seriously.

Roanoke Island

First English colony in the U.S. (1585). Vanished without a trace. In 1587, the first English child born in America was born here — a girl — Virginia Dare.

Although Rhode Island is most famous as the **smallest state** in the Union, we would like to point out that every single man, woman, and child alive in the world today would be able to fit inside the state (so long as they were **all willing to stand**). If that weren't enough, if you carpeted the entire state in dollar bills, something that no one has done yet, but nevertheless, if somebody did, then we are talking approximately **$310 billion.**

Rhode Island has a proud tradition of individual rights. They were founded by refugees seeking religious freedom and they were the first to declare open rebellion against the British in 1776. But they were the **last to ratify the Constitution** (wouldn't do it until the Bill of Rights was added). The state was also home to one of our favorite patriots, Nathanael Green (second in command to George Washington during the Revolutionary War).

Ida Lewis
(1842–1911) So famous in her day for her job as lighthouse keeper (for 55 years) at Lime Rock that she received marriage proposals and even got a visit from President Ulysses S. Grant. In 1924, Lime Rock was renamed Ida Lewis Rock in her honor.

Our Favorite

Most Famous

Mr. Potato Head
(b. 1952) The Hasbro Toy Company of Pawtucket, RI, is the world's biggest toy company and Mr. Potato Head is their guy. The governor of Rhode Island recently named Mr. P. the state's official travel ambassador and a number of 6-foot statues of him were duly installed around the state at tourist spots (where they make tempting targets for college prank spudnappers).

Providence
Home of the "Waterfire," a public art display in which bonfires are set ablaze on platforms mounted out on the Providence River (to a background of appropriately eerie music). It's turned into a huge hit for the city drawing hundreds of thousands to the river's promenade.

Jerimoth Hill

Rhode Island

Providence

Rhode Island

Little Compton

Newport

Succotash Pt.

Little Compton
The state bird is a chicken — the Rhode Island Red. It lays brown eggs.

Providence's biggest fan is Buddy Ciani, the mayor, whose bold career is checkered enough to include a little jail time as well as a successful side job selling the **Mayor's Own Marinara Sauce** (Mom's Sauce). Also, did we mention that Providence manufactures more silverware than anyplace else?

The Blue Bug
A famous sculpture located on the roof of a pest control building in downtown Providence has led many visitors to ask the same question. "In Paris, they may have the Eiffel Tower, but do they have a two-ton termite?" See for yourself: http://www.bluebug.com /history.html

"Careful, bwana, we're in Rhode Island now..." If you'd love to see Africa, but you just don't have the time or money, Rhode Island is where you want to be. Pop over to **Jamestown Island,** just off the RI coast. A part of Jamestown is actually Africa, a bit left behind when the African continent was grinding up against ours 250 million years ago.

Newport
Home of the oldest synagogue in the U.S. (1763).

Succotash Point
Ever wonder what evil mind conceived of succotash, that corn and bean mix that all children fear? Visit Succotash Point, RI, and you will learn all about the Narragansett Indians, originators of the dish. The word "succotash" incidentally, is Narragansett for "vegetable of our revenge." (OK, OK, we made that part up.)

Jerimoth Hill
America's most inaccessible high point. You can talk about Alaska's Denali (20,320 ft) or California's Whitney (14,495 ft) but when adventurers who seek to scale the highest peak in every state gather to share horror stories, Jerimoth Hill in Rhode Island stands alone. It may not be the tallest (812 feet) but the property owner who controls the access to Jerimoth Hill has "No Trespassing" signs every 20 steps and is not a man to be trifled with.

Atlantic Ocean

VERMONT

Vermont leads the nation in **maple sugar** *production. It takes 40 spoonfuls of sap to make one spoonful of maple syrup. Check out the maple sugarhouse web cam at http://www.uvm.edu/~pmrc/sugarcam.html*

Springfield

Justin Morgan, the first Morgan horse, was born here in 1789.

Scrabble tiles

Until 1998, Scrabble tiles were made from Vermont maple. Devoted players memorize long lists of accepted words (often without knowing their meanings) for use in games. For example, **oxyphenbutazone** *will earn you 1,458 points. And don't forget* **maa** *("to bleat as a goat") and* **euk** *("to itch").*

• Burlington

★

Montpelier

Springfield •

Most Famous

CALVIN COOLIDGE

(1872–1933)

30th U.S. president. His nickname was "Silent Cal." Our favorite Coolidge story: A young woman sitting next to Coolidge at a dinner party confided to him she had bet she could get at least three words of conversation from him. Without looking at her he quietly retorted, "You lose."

Montpelier

"Rotten Sneaker Capital of the World" The Odor-Eaters International Rotten Sneaker Contest here is open to kids aged 5–15. Shoes are judged on odor offensiveness, wear on soles, laces and toes. Not that it's related, but Montpelier is also the only state capital without a McDonald's.

Wilson "Snowflake" Bentley

who lived in Jericho, Vermont, photographed over 10,000 snowflakes, no two exactly alike.

Covered bridges

Vermont has **107** of them. A typical 1800s toll for a man on foot was 1 cent; on horseback, 4 cents; a one-horse carriage, 10 cents; drawn by more than one horse, 20 cents; cattle, 1 cent; sheep or swine, a half-cent, and the driver crossed for free. Money collected was used for bridge construction and maintenance.

Burlington

Ben & Jerry's

started in an abandoned gas station. They learned how to make ice cream in a $5 Pennsylvania State correspondence course. Vermont's pigs get to eat the plant's leftovers; they like all the flavors except Mint Oreo.

Kentucky

Most Famous

① Abraham Lincoln

(1809–1865) It's no myth; our finest president was born in a one-room log cabin near Hodgenville, KY.

Jefferson Davis, *by the way, the president of the Confederacy, was also born in Kentucky.*

Louisville ②

The **Kentucky Derby** *is run here every year and has since 1875. It's probably the most expensive two minutes in sport. Louisville was also the home of* **Mildred and Patty Hill**, *who wrote "Happy Birthday" in 1893. The song still earns about* **$2 million** *a year annually. The boxer* **Muhammed Ali**, *born Cassius Clay and for many years the most recognized man on Earth, is from Louisville. Most major league ballplayers, including Mark McGuire and Sammy Sosa, use* **Louisville Slugger bats**. *(There's a museum in town. Look for the* **6-story** *bat.)*

③ Ft. Knox

More than $6 billion in government gold is stored here behind concrete and steel walls. No tours or **samples.**

④ Lexington

Heart of the Bluegrass country and home to a lot of **thoroughbred** *breeding farms. Million-dollar horses with private security guards are not uncommon.*

Frankfort ★

⑤ Bowling Green

All current Chevrolet Corvettes are made in Bowling Green, KY.

⑥ Mammoth Cave National Park *Probably the world's longest cave system is still incompletely mapped — 350 miles and counting.*

⑦ Pikeville

This is McCoy country. The family's famous feud (1860–1890) with the Hatfields of West Virginia apparently started over a stolen pig. These days the families still get together, but the fight's been downgraded to picnics, tug-of-war and softball.

⑧ Corbin

Birthplace of Kentucky Fried Chicken. Col. Harland Sanders, the founder, is buried in Corbin and a museum honoring him and his recipe is also here (where you can see his first frying pan).

Our Favorite

Stephen Bishop

(1780–1850) the greatest explorer of the nation's greatest cave system, Mammoth Caves. Buried near its main entrance.

⑨ Daniel Boone,

the famous explorer, walked into Kentucky in 1775 through the Cumberland Gap.

TENNESSEE

Davey Crockett

(1786–1836). Frontiersman, congressman and defender of the Alamo, Crockett's real life has been hard to make out behind tall tales that have turned him into a kind of comic book hero. He was, truth to tell, a larger-than-life character who mixed politics and frontier expeditions. His ill-fated trip to Texas was prompted by a political defeat. As he told his opponents: "You can go to you know where; I am going to Texas."

Memphis

Check out the Peabody Hotel duck walk. Every day at 11 am a string of ducks leaves their roof-top penthouse, takes the hotel elevator to the lobby, and waddles out the front door. At 5 pm, they go back. Just like clockwork.

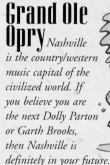

Nashville

Buddy, a female German shepherd, was the first seeing eye dog for a blind person in the U.S.

If you enjoy a well-told story, the National Story Teller's convention is held every year in Murfreesboro, TN.

Tennessee is a great state for caving. One of the state's larger lakes, the Lost Sea, is entirely in a cave; so is a 125-foot waterfall.

Grand Ole Opry

Nashville is the country/western music capital of the civilized world. If you believe you are the next Dolly Parton or Garth Brooks, then Nashville is definitely in your future.

Memphis

Elvis Presley is no longer merely a dead pop star. Elvis is an industry, and it's headquartered here at his mansion Graceland. Elvis recorded his first song in Memphis, he waggled his hips for the first time there and his grave is there. Far more people visit him now that he's dead than ever did when he was alive. In fact, Graceland is the second most popular private residence in the United States, after the White House.

Gibson

has been making guitars of great distinction in Nashville since 1894. This is the Flying V model, like one that Jimi Hendrix played.

Every night, hundreds of **FedEx** planes fly into Memphis, dump all their packages into a huge warehouse where they get shuffled, sorted and reloaded back onto outbound planes by early morning. The whole thing is so amazing that customers regularly show up in the middle of the night to watch the spectacle.

The biggest earthquake in American history was in 1811 and centered in Tennessee. If it happened today, the damage would be off the charts.

Theory of Evolution

One of the most celebrated trials of the 20th century was held in Tennessee in 1925. Called the "Scopes Monkey Trial," it was broadcast live on radio around the country. On trial? The theory of evolution. A high school teacher in Tennessee was teaching it, and the state went to court to stop him.

People in Tennessee have a particular weakness for peanuts, marshmallow and chocolate. At the local

Piggly Wiggly

supermarket chain, you can get a high-calorie dose of all of them in Googoo Clusters or MoonPies, neither of which are health foods. MoonPies were invented in Chattanooga in 1917.

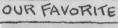

OUR FAVORITE

Wilma Rudolph

(1940–1994). Fastest woman alive in 1960, winner of three Olympic gold medals, all in the sprints. She wore leg braces until the age of 9 because of childhood polio. Her entire life was a class act spent promoting her country, athletics and the cause of racial harmony. One of her teammates put it this way at her funeral: "She was beautiful, she was nice, and she was the best."

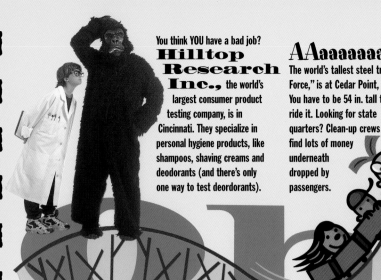

You think YOU have a bad job? **Hilltop Research Inc.,** the world's largest consumer product testing company, is in Cincinnati. They specialize in personal hygiene products, like shampoos, shaving creams and deodorants (and there's only one way to test deordorants).

AAaaaaaaaAAAAaaaaaaah!

The world's tallest steel track roller coaster (310 ft), "Millennium Force," is at Cedar Point, Sandusky, OH. You have to be 54 in. tall to ride it. Looking for state quarters? Clean-up crews find lots of money underneath dropped by passengers.

J🍎hnny Appleseed

was a real person from Mayfield, OH. John Chapman was his name. He really did plant a lot of apple trees.

Hinkley Roost

Every March 15 the buzzards (turkey vultures) return to Hinkley. People in warm coats return to watch them.

• Bryan
• Cleveland
Sandusky
• Canton
Mansfield
• Hinkley
• Newark
Columbus
• Dayton
• Cincinnati

OHIO ART

Bryan. Home of the Etch A Sketch®.

National Soap Box Derby

The first Soap Box Derby was held in Dayton in 1933; 362 kids competed in homemade "anything-that-rolls" cars built from orange crates, baby buggy wheels and other junk. National Derbys are now held in Akron; both boys and girls compete in cars built from official plans. There are lots of rules and no record of a car ever having been built from a soap box.

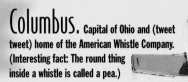

Columbus. Capital of Ohio and (tweet tweet) home of the American Whistle Company. (Interesting fact: The round thing inside a whistle is called a pea.)

Canton
Pro Football Hall of Fame.

Our Favorite

Roy Rogers

(1911–1998) The singing cowboy was born in Cincinnati on second base in Riverfront Stadium. (No, not during a game, but in a house that used to stand there.)

Most Famous

Thomas Edison

(1847–1931) Thomas Edison patented more than a thousand inventions, including the electric lightbulb. Quote: "Genius is one percent inspiration and ninety-nine percent perspiration."

Cleveland: *Home of Chef Boyardee and Lifesavers (invented in 1912) as well as the Rock 'n' Roll Hall of Fame where you can see John Lennon's report card and Jim Morrison's Cub Scout uniform. Cleveland also had the first stoplight (1914).*

Newark
Home of the Longaberger Basket Company. That's its building in the photograph.

17

Louisiana

Most Famous

Louis Armstrong (1901–1971)

Jazz musician (trumpet). His nickname "Satchmo" was short for Satchelmouth.

One *of the few places where you can* **bite a gator** *(in a restaurant).*

All of Louisiana has been, at one time or another, at the bottom of the Mississippi River.

Nutria

Population explosion. Eat one today! They taste like rabbit.

Our Favorite

Mahalia Jackson

(1911–1972) Gospel singer since the age of five when she began belting it out in her father's church. Quote: "Don't need any microphone. Just open the doors and windows."

Bonnie and Clyde, Depression era bank robbers, shot here on May 23, 1934. Re-enactments yearly.

Lake Peigneur went spinning down the drain on November 20, 1980. It was located over a salt mine into which an oil drilling rig punched a hole. Also sucked down: 2 oil rigs, 11 barges, a mobile home, a parking lot, botanical gardens and a bunch of other stuff. Amazingly, the salt miners made it out.

Superdome

Largest room in the world without pillars. 384,024,577.5 footballs would fit inside.

New Orleans

Great **voodoo** town. Largest city in the Confederacy.

The **Battle of New Orleans,** *fought two weeks after the end of the War of 1812, made* **Andrew Jackson** *a national hero. The pirate* **Jean Lafitte** *helped him.*

Avery Island Good place to grow chiles. Home to Tabasco Sauce since 1868.

Cajun Country has its own language, music and Zydeco style.

The Higgins boat, the ramp-fronted landing craft used on D-Day in World War II, was invented and built in New Orleans.

INDIANA

1 Clarksville

Where the Lewis and Clark expedition took its first step on October 23, 1803.

2 South Bend

The Studebaker Brothers Manufacturing Company made conestoga wagons before they made classy cars. See both at the Studebaker National Museum.

Our Favorite

Twyla Tharp, (b. 1941),

one of the most influential dancers and dance choreographers of the past 50 years, is an Indianian.

3 Santa Claus

Send a holiday card there this Christmas and they'll postmark it for you. Address it to: The Big Red Guy, Jingle Bells Lane, Santa Claus IN 47479.

Most Famous
Larry Bird

(b. 1956), basketball superstar, has a street named after him in his little hometown of French Lick, IN. (But in 1981, 1984 and 1986 when he led the Celtics to the national championship, they probably could have re-named the whole state after him.)

★ Indianapolis

Approximately 70,000 people attend the Super Bowl every year; the Indianapolis 500 motorcar race draws 250,000. (Winning speed? About 167 mph.) In a slightly slower vein, Indianapolis is also the home of the largest children's museum in the United States, as well as the birthplace of Wonder Bread and Raggedy Ann.

4 Fountain City

Levi and Catherine Coffin's house in Fountain City was the Grand Central Station of the Underground Railroad in the days before the Civil War. Thousands of escaped slaves were hidden there en route to freedom.

5 Bloomington Little 500

A one-speed bicycle race on a cinder track. Rent Breaking Away for Hollywood's version of the famous race.

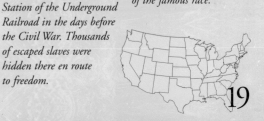

19

M-I-S-S-I-S-S-I-P-P-I

Some say that the people make the place and, in the case of Mississippi, it's true. So many good people *are from the state that we couldn't chose a single famous and favorite.* **Our yearbook includes:**

Brandy *(b. 1979)*

Singer and TV star. Hobbies = going to the mall, hanging out with friends, reading, watching basketball and cleaning her room.

BRETT FAVRE

(b. 1969) The famous Green Bay Packers' quarterback grew up in Kiln (pronounced Kill), MS, where his dad was his coach. Shares the NFL record for longest pass completion.

Medgar Evers **(1925–1963)**

Civil Rights leader. His murder pushed President John F. Kennedy to introduce a Civil Rghts bill banning segregation.

B.B. King

(b. 1925) King of the Blues. B.B. stands for Blues Boy. In the 1950s he saved his $30 guitar from a fire caused by a fight over a woman named Lucille, then named the guitar after her.

Our Favorite Oprah Winfrey

(b. 1954) TV talk show host, philanthropist, and movie star and one of the richest women in the U.S. She began her "broadcasting career" at the age of three by reading aloud. We like her for her efforts to encourage reading.

Most Famous Elvis Presley

(1935–1977) His image appears on more tacky objects than anyone else in history. Who would you rather have dinner with — early/skinny Elvis or older/large and sequined Elvis? But seriously, he was a really good singer.

William Faulkner

(1897–1962) Nobel Prize — winning novelist known for his portrayal of the American South. His characters like the descendants of old families, carpet-baggers, swamp rats, farm hands, bootleggers and peddlers are legendary.

Jackson

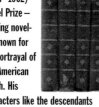

Jerry Rice

(b. 1962) The greatest receiver in NFL history. He formed a powerhouse passing combination with quarterback Joe Montana.

LeAnn Rimes

(b. 1982) The pop star started singing at age 2, won a song and dance contest at age 5 (she sang "Getting to Know You"), and recorded her first album at age 11. She's won two Grammys. Rimes lists her #1 hobby as shopping.

Muddy Waters

(1915–1983) The famous blues guitarist's real name was McKinley Morganfield. With songs like "Hoochie Coochie Man" and "Got My Mojo Working" he had much to do with establishing the modern Chicago blues sound.

ILLINOIS

Walt Disney,
(1901–1966) former WWII ambulance driver, later started a children's cartoon company. First talking animated character? Mickey Mouse. He built Disneyland, incidentally, despite the advice of basically everybody in his company.

◉ De Kalb
Barbed wire, which put an end to the free range of the American West and later cost thousands of lives in WWI, was invented here.

◉ Aledo
Townspeople invented the name by pulling letters out of a hat.

It's true.
Twinkies were invented in Illinois. In an experiment we accidentally conducted ourselves, Twinkies do not support insect life or change in appearance after 6 weeks of being outside on a picnic table.

◉ Collinsville
Yes, this is the home of the nation's largest catsup bottle. (www.catsupbottle.com for those of you who doubt).

◉ Metropolis
Superman's hometown.

The Tully Monster
(Tullimonstrum gregarium) is the Illinois State Fossil. The now-extinct creature was a soft-bodied marine animal with teeth. It lived 300 million years ago and was unique to Illinois.

Edgar Rice Burroughs,
(1875–1950) who never visited Africa in his life, created Tarzan and wrote 28 books of the apeman's adventures. He was, for many years, the answer to the question: Who has more books in print than any writer in the world?

◉ Kickapoo
Our very favorite town name in the entire United States of America.

✦ Springfield
Abraham Lincoln, generally acknowleged to be the nation's greatest president, practiced law in this part of Illinois for 23 years. He's buried here.

Bessie Coleman,
the first African-American woman to earn a pilot's license, lived in Illinois.

◉ Oakbrook
Home to McDonald's Hamburger U., where one can take courses like Advanced Burger Flipping and Introductory French Fries.

◉ Chicago
Home of the Sears Tower, the tallest building in the United States (climbed to the top, incidentally, by a guy using suction cups in 1981).

21

ALABAMA

OUR FAVORITE
Mae Jemison

(b. 1956) Our favorite Alabaman is a Stanford graduate, chemical engineer, Peace Corp veteran, medical doctor, and, as of August 1992, a flight-tested astronaut. ❶ She was born in Decatur.

Y'all Come Back Now

❷ *Alabamans in Huntsville built the Saturn 5 booster rocket that lifted Neil Armstrong, Michael Collins and Buzz Aldrin on the first leg of their trip to the moon in 1969.*

St. Bear

Bear Bryant is Alabama's patron saint. He's the former coach of the University of Alabama's football team, the Crimson Tide. In Alabama, the rivalry between the Tide and Clemson (Clemson, AL) is taken far more seriously than human tongues can tell.

22

③ Tuscumbia

The hometown of **Helen Keller,** *Harvard graduate, author, speaker, political activist, recipient of the Presidential Medal of Freedom and member of the National Institute of Arts. Blind and deaf from the age of two.*

④ The Home of Atticus, Scout and Jem

Harper Lee, the author of To Kill a Mockingbird, *grew up in Monroeville, AL, a town she recalled when she created the fictional "Maycomb County" of her famous novel.*

There's Bad Luck, and then there's BAD Luck. Only one person in the history of the United States has ever been **officially hit by a meteorite**. ⑤ It happened in Sylacauga, AL. Mrs. E. Hulitt Hodge was in her sitting room in 1954 when a meteorite came through her roof and bounced off her hip.

Tuskegee Institute

⑥ Training ground of the famed Tuskegee Airmen, an African American fighter group of 450 pilots that saw action in Italy and Africa during World War II.

MOST FAMOUS
Henry Louis Aaron

(b. 1934) The number is 755. That's how many homers Hank Aaron hit in his career, number one on the list. Babe Ruth is a distant second. You could look it up.

Hey, That's MY Bag!

⑦ *Many of the U.S. airlines dispose of their unclaimed baggage by sending it to an outlet in Scottsboro, AL. When you get really desperate, check out* **unclaimed baggage.com.**

★ Montgomery

On the afternoon of December 1, 1955, Rosa Parks, an African American woman, declined to yield her seat to a white passenger on a Montgomery city bus. That refusal, and a subsequent boycott of the Montgomery buses led by the Reverend Martin Luther King, Jr., is often called the trigger to the entire U.S. Civil Rights movement.

MAINE

Stephen King

(b. 1947) King of horror writing and the world's most successful writer with over a hundred million copies of his work in print.

Folks who live in Maine are called "down-easters" and they include Charlotte and Wilbur, the literate spider and radiant pig in E.B. White's book *Charlotte's Web*, which he wrote at his salt water farm near ● Blue Hill.

Leon L. Bean invented the rubber-bottom, leather-top hunting boot. He also founded the world-famous L.L. Bean store which has turned the (formerly) quiet little town of ● Freeport into Maine's top tourist attraction.

Maine is the kind of state that has 1,253,000 people and 30,000 moose. Visitors who look at all like moose are cautioned against roaming the woods during hunting season.

"If the hunters don't get ya, the blackflies will."

more than 5,000 lakes

Maine coon cat

33 USA

AUGUSTA ★

Louis Sockalexis

(1871-1913) Grandson of a Penobscot chief and the first full-blooded Native American to play Major League Baseball (for Cleveland).

When you get away from the coast of Maine, you get into its back country, home to lots of funny-named summer camps. Our favorite?

Camp Waziyatah

At daybreak on January 1, 2000, the summit of ● Mt. Cadillac in Acadia National Park was crowded with freezing people wanting to be the first on American soil to see the new millenium dawn. This peak is where the sun rises first every day in America.

Maine's coastline and islands are world famous, as are its lighthouses, blueberries, lobsters, sardines and hunting boots.

pincher claw   crusher claw

Chester Greenwood, an inventor from ● Farmington, created the first pair of earmuffs in 1873.

Missouri

The Pony Express *started in* ⑦ St. Joseph.

Yogi Berra

(b. 1925) Great baseball catcher and hard-to-strike-out hitter. Some famous quotations: "It ain't over 'til it's over." "I usually take a two-hour nap from one to four." "It's deja vu all over again." "The future ain't what it used to be." "You can observe a lot by watching." "Never answer an anonymous letter." "It gets late early out here."

① Branson

is the country's **Country Music theme town**, *where the show is non-stop.*

Mark Twain, a.k.a. Samuel Clemens

(1835–1910) American humorist, riverboat pilot, gold prospector, journalist and storyteller. His name comes from a Mississippi River phrase meaning "two fathoms deep" (a safe depth for a steamboat). Among our favorites of his books: *The Adventures of Tom Sawyer* (1876); *The Prince and the Pauper* (1882); *Life on the Mississippi* (1883); *The Adventures of Huckleberry Finn* (1884); *Pudd'nhead Wilson* (1884); and *A Connecticut Yankee in King Arthur's Court* (1889).

② *Clemens grew up in* **Hannibal,** *right on the river, a fact that's impossible to miss if you visit today. There's a Mark Twain Hotel, Mark Twain Dinette, Mark Twain Roofing Company, the Mark Twain Solid Waste District and...well, you get the picture.*

St. Louis is **the largest city** *in Missouri, but the capital is* ③ **Jefferson City.**

④ **St. Louis**
The city has several claims to fame: ● *first (successful)* **parachute jump** *from an airplane (1912),* ● *first* **7-UP** *(originally called Bib-Label Lithiated Lemon-Lime Soda, (1929) and,* ● *first well-documented case of frogs raining from the sky (1873).*

⑤ **Lamar** *is the birthplace of former president Harry S. Truman. When he lived there, his home had no electricity, running water, clothes closets or bathroom. Not only that, his middle initial "S" doesn't stand for anything.*

St. Louis' **630-ft** *Gateway Arch (designed with pipe-cleaners).*

The largest underground business complex in the world is located in ⑥ **Kansas City**. *The SubTropolis was mined out of a 270-million-year-old limestone deposit and covers 2,500 acres. The space is used for cold storage, warehousing and the like. Both trucks and trains can drive inside.*

ARKANSAS

Hardest state to spell and pronounce, but one of the best for gearing up for low-tech self-protection since it's home to the **Daisy Air Gun Company** (Rogers), the country's **largest bow and arrow manufacturer** (Pine Bluff), and its **first Bowie knife maker** (in Washington, AR). And, if you should need any ducks or fish to come to your aid, Arkansas is also the country's **leading supplier of duck calls** (Stuttgart, AR) as well as artificial bass lures. **Bass fishing,** incidentally, is a big deal in Arkansas and live television coverage of profes-sional bass fishing is not uncommon.

Arkansas is a state of small towns. *Even the capital,* **Little Rock,** *doesn't have a big city feel (its skyline is dominated by the 41-story T.C.B.Y. frozen yogurt building).* Our favorite Arkansas little town names? Greasy Corner, Ozone, Bald Knob, Snowball, Waldo, Possum Grape, and Whistleville. Your job? Find Waldo. *(Your other job is to stop in at the* Arkansas Alligator Farm and Petting Zoo *in Hot Springs, AR, and tell us what it was like.)*

Most Famous Bill Clinton
(b. 1946) *The 42nd president of the United States was born in Hope, Arkansas, a town also famous for* **gigantic watermelons.**

Our Favorite DizzyDean
(1910–1974) A Hall of Fame pitcher whose skill in baseball was equalled only by his command of the language ("The doctors x-rayed my head and found nothing").

One town, Texarkana, *is located square on the Texas-Arkansas border. The line runs right down the main street and Texas police patrol one lane, while the Arkansas state troopers handle the other.*

Another town, **Bentonville,** is the headquarters of the world's largest retail chain, **Wal-Mart,** where every hour, among many other things, they sell 11,645 large boxes of diapers.

A third town, Murfreesboro, is home to the **Crater of Diamonds State Park,** *where* visitors are allowed to take samples home *provided they can dig them up themselves.*

If Arkansas had a state religion, it would be football, specifically the form practiced by the University of Arkansas Razorbacks team and if you cannot throw your head back and holler **"WOOO OOOPig SOOOOOO OOOOOIEE!"** then you are just not from Arkansas. It's that simple.

25

Michigan

Folks in the upper part of the state call themselves "Uppers" (pronounced "you-pers") and often joke about forming their own state. Michigan is known as "The Wolverine State," but none of the animals live there.

Upper Michigan

Water

Native Americans called the region Kitchigummi which (in addition to being fun to say) means Great Water. The state is surrounded on three sides by Great Lakes. (That's a lot of fresh water — 6 quadrillion gallons to be exact. Only Lake Baikal in Siberia and the polar ice caps contain more.) *In Michigan you are never more than 6 miles from a lake or more than 85 miles from a Great Lake.*

If you live in the lower peninsula of Michigan you can show people just where by pointing to a spot on your hand; that part of the state's shaped like a mitten.

Grand Rapids
Battle Creek
Lansing
Vicksburg
Cassopolis
Colon
Detroit

Our Favorite
Ervin "Magic" Johnson

(b. 1959) He was known as "June Bug" as a kid. A sportswriter impressed by Johnson's skills on the basketball court dubbed him "Magic." He's considered one of the greatest point guards and playmakers in NBA history.

Most Famous
Henry Ford

(1863–1947)

The maker of Ford cars and inventor of the modern assembly line also invented charcoal briquets.

Cars

One-third of the nation's cars are manufactured in Michigan. Luckily, about 25 old cars are taken off the road and recycled every minute in the U.S. 97.9% of the steel used to make new cars comes from old cars. Another car fact: There's enough energy in a tank of gas to lift a car into orbit.

Michigan
The Wolverine State

Cassopolis

Kitty Litter was invented here.

Detroit

Motown music started in The Motor City. Visit Greenfield Village to see the chair in which Lincoln was shot, as well as the Wright Brothers' bicycle shop and Thomas Edison's lab — all, by the way, moved here from other states.

Battle Creek

W.K. and John Harvey Kellogg first created their cereal for the patients of The Battle Creek Sanitarium. The brothers believed that eating grains kept folks "regular" (if you know what we mean) and started selling cereal to the public in 1906. You can tour the factory. Post Cereals was also founded here (1895).

Grand Rapids

A good place to call home. The carpet sweeper (1876), the bread slicer (1932), President Gerald R. Ford and Amway all come from Grand Rapids. Grand Rapids is also number one in the consumption of Spaghetti-Os. Incidentally, there really is a rapids and the town's on the Grand River.

Colon

It was named for a river that resembled a (ahem) colon (not punctuation), but is famous as the "Magic Capital of the World." Good magic stores.

Vicksburg

First Elvis Sighting (four days after his death). Somebody saw him in Felpausch's Supermarket. No word on what was in his cart. Someone else saw him at Burger King in Kalamazoo; he was driving a red Ferrari.

Florida

Most Famous Floridian

JIM MORRISON. *Frenzied, hyper-kinetic lead singer of the rock group The Doors, Morrison died the "rock star's death" in Paris at the age of 28. So many pilgrims visit his grave there every year that the traffic has become a sore point for other families visiting the cemetery.*

Our Favorite Floridian

THE MANATEE. With looks that only a mother could love, the famed Florida sea cows are being loved to death by sightseeing tourists in motorboats whose propellors are killing the gentle sea mammals.

Bunnell.

High school graduating student Duane Tucker never missed a day of school. 2,340 days in a row. This could be the most amazing record we've ever heard of.

The state of Florida is **made up almost entirely of dead bodies.** *They belonged to single-celled sea animals that died millions of years ago. The end result makes for a huge, low-lying peninsula with great swamps, lakes and sinkholes but not much in the way of mountain ranges. In fact, the tallest point in the state is Britton Hill,* **only 345 feet high.** *Just finding it is a big challenge for all the adventurers who set out every year to climb the tallest peak in every state.*

Loggerhead sea turtles.

These graceful reptiles are a Threatened Species due to the overharvest of their eggs for food, accidental drownings in commercial fishing nets and intentional death inflicted for their skin or shells.

Howey-in-the-Hills.

Wayne and Marty Scott manufacture the **finest clown shoes** *in the country here. Size 34 is a "small." $220 a pair and worth it.*

Lantana.

Did you ever wonder where they write those fabulous headlines on grocery store newspapers? Things like, **"Woman Gives Birth to Twin Baboons"** *or* **"I Was Abducted by Elvis at the Wheel of a U.F.O."** *Both the* **National Enquirer** *and the* **Weekly World News** *are published in Lantana, FL.*

Cape Canaveral

Cape Canaveral, FL, is where every manned American space flight launches. NASA doesn't like the hurricanes, but they need to launch over water...just in case.

Miami.

Although we do not normally include things like Official State Songs— in the case of Florida, the state with more senior citizens than any other — we will make an exception. Florida's official state song is "Old Folks at Home."

Gatorade was developed at the University of Florida and named after the Gators, a thirsty bunch of football players.

Tallahassee

Bunnell •

Howey-in-the-Hills •

Orlando •

Cape Canaveral

Lantana •

Fort Lauderdale •

Estero •

Miami •

If alligator wrestling is a career interest of yours, you should know that Florida dominates the industry. Gatorland, in Orlando, has been staging **gator versus human wrestling matches** since long before Disney got there. And at Okalee Indian Village, a competing venue, they offer frequent employment opportunities for gator rasslers ($12 an hour, no experience necessary but quick hands are an asset).

Orlando.

More pictures are taken at Walt Disney World, the world's number one tourist attraction, than at any other single location on the planet.

Lake Okeechobee.

Worst Alligators. 14.5 ft. long!

Fort Lauderdale.

This is where East Coast college students migrate to celebrate spring break every year. A true parental nightmare.

Estero, FL.

Dr. Cyrus Teed founded a religious commune here in 1894 that believed, among other things, that the world was hollow and people lived insde of it. The commune survived for many years and you can still take tours of the compound.

Texas

There are a few key facts that you need to know in order to really understand Texas, a state so big that it would take 28,411,648,830,000 people to eat it (assuming it was a pancake). Here, we believe, are the essentials:

Our Favorite
Red Adair *(b. 1915) A good guy to have at a big fire. His company is famous for controlling oil well fires, including one called the "Devil's Cigarette Lighter" in the Sahara Desert (1962) and others in Kuwait at the end of Operation Desert Storm (1991).*

Lubbock *is the hometown of the original rock and roller* **Buddy Holly** *who called his band "The Crickets." (Years later, an English band that admired him a lot called themselves "The Beatles.")*

A Stonehenge display of tails-up Cadillacs half-buried in the ground on Route 66 near Amarillo.

Created in Waco, 1885. What's the secret behind the taste of Dr. Pepper? We'll never know. They keep the recipe in a vault.

These days in **San Antonio** *you can also see* **Barney Smith's Toilet Seat museum,** *where you can view over 500 hand-decorated toilet seats. In* **Plano,** *there exists the* **Texas Cockroach Hall of Fame** *where the largest Texan is 4" long.*

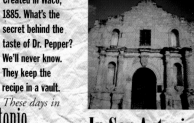

In San Antonio, *you can find the famous* **Alamo,** *hallowed ground in Texas where glorious defenders Davy Crockett and Jim Bowie died at the hands of General Santa Anna's Mexican army. The general later went on to play an important role in the invention of* **bubble gum,** *while the man who popularized the fighting cry "Remember the Alamo" later invented* **condensed milk.**

Austin, the state capital,
is where you'll find the famed U of T as well as an **enormous population of urban bats** and the source of all those Dell Computers (Austin is Texas's "Silicon Range"). If you're visiting on the Fourth of July, when the city's Spam Festival is on, be sure to try the "Spam Foo Yung."

Just outside of Corpus Christi—
Refugio, to be precise — is where Nolan Ryan is from, one of the most dominant and enduring baseball pitchers of the past 50 years.

Houston,
the country's leading dog-bite town, as well as the first word spoken from the surface of the moon, was also the hometown of **Miss Ima Hogg,** *one of the city's wealthiest society ladies and* **Daughter of Governor James Stephen Hogg** *(who named his daughter Ima in order to see if wealth could make up for ANYTHING).*

In Houston,
the country's largest Art Car parade takes place every summer, drawing over 200,000 spectators and several hundred hand-decorated "wheeled entries."

In Malakoff, there's a guy who can perform the University of Texas fight song with a hand under his armpit.

Fort Worth

Austin

San Antonio

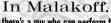

In Ft. Worth, they print dollar bills all day long at the mint's western manufacturing plant. *Employees are asked to carry their lunches in clear plastic bags to "prevent confusion."*

Visiting Fort Worth? Stop by **The National Cowgirl Museum and Hall of Fame.**

Barney is a Texan. So, for that matter, is **Stone Cold Steve Austin.**

Larry McMurtry,
the famed author of *Lonesome Dove, The Last Picture Show,* etc., is using his money to turn his hometown of **Archer City** into the country's largest "booktown" with zillions of books for sale on a street full of new and used bookstores.

Most Famous
Sandra Day O'Connor *(b. 1930) First female U.S. Supreme Court justice.*

IOWA

Grant Wood (1892–1942)
Painter from Iowa famous for landscapes and especially for his painting *American Gothic*.

The birthplace of Cracker Jacks and Eskimo Pies,
Iowa is a great state for looking at cornfields (Don't believe us? Check them out at iowafarmer.com/corncam/corn.html). If you'd like to do it in person, we recommend the Ragbrae, the annual bike race across the whole state. Ten thousand riders going from town to town, homemade pies all the way.

Forest City. *All those* **Winnebago motorhomes** *start their long journeys right at the Winnebago factory.*

Laurens
Forest City
Clear Lake
Waterloo
West Branch
Muscatine
Council Bluffs
Des Moines

Waterloo,
Tractor-town. Largest John Deere factory in the world. Tractor square-dancing in Nemaha.

Muscatine.
There used to be over 100 button factories here.

Des Moines, *the leading Jell-O consuming city in the world.*

Laurens. In 1994,
73-year-old Alvin Straight left on his John Deere ride-on lawnmower for a 5 mph personal odyssey *to see his ailing brother in Mt. Zion, WI, 240 miles away. Rent* The Straight Story *for a beautiful telling of a great story.*

Council Bluffs. *Hometown to David Yort. (He's the blue Power Ranger.) Also, an unrelated item, the Commercial Bluff jail has a* **man-sized hamster cage** *for inmates with time to pass.*

Clear Lake.
Buddy Holly, Richie Valens and the Big Bopper were passengers in an airplane that crashed just outside of Clear Lake, IA, on February 3, 1959, **"the day the music died."** *Every year, people come from around the world to a concert staged in town on the anniversary of the wreck.*

Ann Landers (b. 1918) and **Dear Abby**
(a.k.a. Abigail Van Buren, b. 1918). The two advice columnists aren't just sisters, they're twins from the town of Sioux City. After a combined 89 years of dispensing advice, they have the country's ear. If either one of them recommends a book, for example, sales will skyrocket (hint, hint).

West Branch.
Birthplace of Herbert Hoover (1st president born west of the Mississippi). *He's also buried here.* Herb (cat) *lives in a little replica of his birthplace.*

Wisconsin

Wisconsin is the land of milk, cheese and cheeseheads — unique foam headdresses often found at sporting events. *Mention something dairy and you're likely to find it in Wisconsin.* The first ice cream sundae, for example, was made in **Two Rivers** (1881). *A large portion of the population are of German descent, making it a good state in which to eat a sausage.* Sheboygan *holds an annual Bratwurst Eating Contest. The winner gets a trophy with a pig on top.*

Sayner
Milwaukee claims the Harley, Sayner the snowmobile. The first one was built in 1925 by Carl Eliason who rigged a toboggan with tracks and attached a gas engine.

Luck
Once home to the **Duncan Yo-Yo Factory** because of the abundance of maple wood from which the toys were made. (Also a lucky place to live — yuck yuck...)

Eagle River
In 1961, Joe Simonton, a plumber here, filled a jug of water for the UFO that hovered over his yard. In return he received four "space cookies" which professors at Northwestern University determined contained flour, sugar and grease — just like Earth cookies.

Hayward
National Freshwater Fishing Hall of Fame
World's largest fiberglass fish, a muskie. 1/2 city block long and five stories high.

Milwaukee
Harley-Davidson
started here; engines and transmissions for many models are still made here. Number of bikes made in the first year of operation: 3. Price: under $300. Cost today: $11,000 or more. Also invented here: the typewriter (1873 — Mark Twain owned one of the first models and wrote Life on the Mississippi *on it) and the outboard motor (Ole Evinrude, 1907).*

Madison
State capital. Bikes outnumber people here 3 to 2.

Georgia O'Keeffe
(1887–1986) *Renowned painter of bones, flowers and the land.*

Baraboo
In addition to having a great name, the town is home to the Circus World Museum where you can see over 200 huge circus wagons (displayed in a pavilion the size of a football field), a costume made for the world's smallest man, flea circus props and funhouse mirrors.

Harry Houdini
(1874–1926) *Born in Hungary but raised in Wisconsin, Houdini was a master at getting out of tough spots such as wrapped in chains and dropped in the sea, suspended upside down in a straightjacket, or locked in a trunk. He distrusted other magicians and spiritualists, attributing his feats to skill and freely explaining how many of his tricks were performed.*

Manitowoc
In 1962, a 21-pound fragment of the Soviet satellite Sputnik IV landed at the intersection of Park and North 8th Street. Nobody was hurt.

Map labels: Sayner • Eagle River • Luck • Two Rivers • Manitowoc • Sheboygan • Baraboo • Madison • Milwaukee

California is only a single state by accident. If North America were flipped, and the Pilgrims had landed in California first, California would be at least five states. **Berkeley** would be its own country; **Hollywood** its own planet.

AMY TAN (b. 1952) Author who writes about mothers, daughters and the Chinese American experience. She never goes anywhere without her dog, Mr. Zo, and sometimes sings with a rock band, The Rock Bottom Remainders.

We live in California so we cannot be objective, but we believe there are **4,144,091,88** amazing things about California. Here are just a few of our favorites:

Bullwinkle *was born in California; so were* **mountain biking**, **skateboarding**, **windsurfing**, POPSICLES, peanut butter, **Frisbees**, **Candyland** *and the* **integrated circuit**.

The **American Flat Earth Society** has its headquarters located in California. So does the nation's largest matador school.

THE LOWEST POINT *in the country is in Death Valley, CA. So is the best hang gliding, rock climbing and* **kayaking.**

The **Apple** *Computer Company is located in California, so is* **Legoland**, **Disneyland**

The Los Angeles Yellow Pages contains 75 listings under **"Personal Trainer."**

There are more **Ferraris** sold in California than all the other states combined.

One *out of every* **eight** *Americans lives in California;* **one** *out of every* **two hundred** *Californians is in jail.*

More Californians believe they have been **abducted by aliens** than residents of any other state.

Charlie Chaplin *used to live in California, so did* **Jack London**, **L. Frank Baum,** *and the guy who mistakenly took a plane to* **Auckland,** *New Zealand when he was trying to go to* **Oakland, CA.**

On the world wide web, a Google search under **"California"** yields **11,493,934** results, and counting; search **"United States"** and you'll get a mere **3,411,100.**

Skywalker Ranch, and the main group behind the Search for Extraterrestrial Intelligence (S.E.T.I.).

California leads the nation in **artichoke** production.

Last but not least… Palo Alto, CA, is the famed **galactic headquarters** *of Klutz. Check us out at* **klutz.com**

Charlie Chaplin

JACK LONDON (1876–1916) Seeker of adventure and writer. The author of *White Fang* and *The Call of the Wild,* also lived as a railroad hobo, oyster pirate, gold prospector, and journalist.

Minnesota

Our Favorite

Paul Bunyan

Half the towns in Minnesota claim to be the birthplace of this folk giant. The following have statues: Akeley, Bloomington, Beminji, Brainerd, and Chisholm. See Paul Bunyan's grave in Kelliher, his anchor in Ortonville, his rifle in Blackduck, and a statue of his girlfriend, Lucette Diana Kensack, in Hackensack.

Walnut Grove

The childhood home of writer Laura Ingalls Wilder, the author of The Little House on the Prairie *series. It's described in* On the Banks of Plum Creek.

Le Sueur

Birthplace of the Jolly Green Giant (a good friend of Betty Crocker's, a Minneapolis gal).

LAKE Wobegon

America's most popular small town. Home of Norwegian bachelor farmers and above-average children. However, you won't find it on the map; it was invented by writer and radio personality Garrison Keillor.

Bloomington

Mall of America. The largest covered shopping mall in the U.S. of A. with over 500 stores.

Legend has it that **Babe,** Paul Bunyan's animal companion, created Minnesota's many lakes with his feet while tromping around the woods. Great canoeing country if you can time your trip to miss the mosquitoes.

Hibbing,

heart of the iron country. This part of Minnesota is actually displaced Canada. It was pushed into place by glaciers during the last ice age.

Hibbing

Minneapolis St Paul

Bloomington
Le Sueur
Walnut Plainview
Grove

Blue Austin
Earth

Plainview
Home of Polly the Cow, famous for successfully predicting the results of five presidential races (1972–1988) by precision pooping. Her owner prepared a "ballot" by spreading pictures of the candidates in her pen. Since this is a family publication, we will not describe the way Polly votes.

Blue Earth
Home of the first ice cream sandwich.

Bob Dylan

(b. 1941) Born Robert Zimmerman, the singer adopted his stage name in honor of Welsh poet Dylan Thomas. Dylan wrote "Mr. Tamborine Man" and many other songs so popular you're likely to hear them today in elevators.

Austin

Spamtown USA. They host a yearly festival where you can try Spam Tacos, Sweet and Sour Spam and Spam Cheese Curds. Opening soon: The Spam Museum.

SPAM

Minneapolis/ St. Paul

Home of the Pillsbury Doughboy. Rollerblades were invented here (1980) by hockey-playing brothers Scott and Brennan Olson. 3M is located here and responsible for such how-did-we-ever-get-along-without-its as: Scotch Tape (1930), Post-it Notes (1980), and Scotchgard (invented by a woman, Patsy Sherman, 1955).

OREGON

If you don't mind getting rained on, Oregon (which probably comes from the French word for hurricane) is a good state for you. The coast has maybe the best beachcombing in the country; freighters often lose cargo in the mid-Pacific and some great stuff washes ashore. They once found a cannon in Cannon Beach. You can also find Japanese glass fishing floats. If you spend time in the woods, however, watch your back. The legendary Sasquatch or Big Foot reportedly lives in the Columbia River Valley. Southwest Oregon has the largest concentration of black bears in the United States.

Portland *("The Rose City"). Home to View-Master, Hacky Sack and Nike (70% of running shoe owners use them for walking only), it's the only city in the U.S. with a volcano within the city limits. The annual Ducky Derby features thousands of duckies dropped from a truck into the Willamette River. Hopefully, they race downstream; sometimes they don't.*

Most Famous
Matt Groening
(b. 1954) Creator of The Simpsons. Marge and Homer are named after his parents. As a student his doodling often got him sent to the principal's office. Look where it got him. (P.S. It's pronounced "graining.")

Our Favorite
Beverly Cleary
(b. 1916) Creator of Beezus and Ramona, Henry Huggins and a slew of other characters, Cleary grew up in a town so small it had no library and writing for young readers was her childhood ambition. "I wanted to write funny stories about the sort of children I knew."

Portland • Boring
Lincoln City
Jacksonville • Crater Lake
Ashland •

ROSE FESTIVAL 1935 JUNIOR MEMBER

Crater Lake
Created by the eruption of Mount Mazama about 7,700 years ago. It's the deepest lake in the world. While this volcano is dormant, your best chance of catching a live one in action is southeast of Bend — Newberry Crater.

Lincoln City
Once home of Keiko the whale (the inspiration for "Free Willie" now lives in Iceland) and a good spot to fly kites or go kite buggy racing (a sport that involves hitching a kite to a wheeled buggy).

Jacksonville
Birthplace of **Bozo the Clown** *(His real name was Pinto Kolvig.)*

Ashland
Major center for Shakespeare performance.

Oregon Trail
The famous trail was the only practical route to the western U.S. for early settlers as it afforded the only route over the mountains. 1840–1860 were the heavily traveled years. Trail life wasn't easy. 12,000 travelers died from disease and accident; 350 from Indian attacks.

Boring
Possibly our favorite U.S. town name. But seriously folks, there's lots to do in Oregon as evidenced by this photo of the Harney County Sagebrush Orchestra (1915).

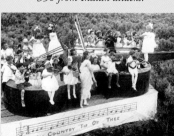

33

KANSAS

The **first American in outer space** *was from Kansas. (That would be Miss Able, a chimpanzee.)*

Kansas is the kind of place you can find things like **Einstein's brain** (Wichita; kept in a jar) as well as Comanche, a horse and the only non–Native American survivor of Custer's Last Stand (Lawrence; stuffed on a stand).

Kansas *didn't legalize the sale of liquor in restaurants until 1978. Before then, when jetliners flew over the state, the flight attendants had to stop serving drinks.*

Lebanon
Dead center of the U.S. This is where the country would balance on your fingertip.

Topeka
Dr. Samuel ("Swat") Crumbine, inventor of the modern fly-swatter (1905), worked in Kansas.

Atchison
The birthplace of Amelia Earhart.

Topeka

OREGON TRAIL

Emporia

Francisco Coronado

The Spanish explorer started in Mexico on a quest for the fabled Seven Gold Cities of Cibola in 1540. Kansas is where he quit.

Wichita, *KS, is where most of the private airplanes you see flying around are made. Ditto for all the Coleman lanterns. The last high school kid to break the 4-minute mile was from Wichita, Jim Ryun, in 1964.*

Coffeyville *ICEE machine invented by Omar Kredlik 1961 — it was the first frozen carbonated drink machine.*

Dodge City used to be a railhead town where a lot of cattle drives finished up. The legendary **Marshall Wyatt Earp** *kept the peace there for a while in the 1870s.*

Kansas is probably best known as the place where **Dorothy wasn't anymore** *when she went to Oz by tornado. As you might have guessed, a "Land of Oz" theme park is being built outside Kansas City (complete with yellow brick road).*

Our favorite random Kansas fact? The 1987 film **NiceGirls Don't Explode** *was filmed here.*

James Naismith,
the inventor of basketball, is from Kansas. He coached at Kansas U. for a while (the only coach there to retire with a losing record).

Buster Keaton
(1895–1966) Silent film comedian whose deadpan expressions, acrobatic skills and great timing make his films timeless classics. Rent *The General* for his best film.

Big Brutus, *a 16-story steam shovel, is retired and on display in West Mineral.*

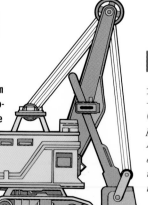

Amelia Earhart
(1897–1937) First female pilot to fly solo over the Atlantic. Her plane disappeared on a later trip while she was attempting to circumnavigate the world.

34

West Virginia

General Thomas Jonathan "Stonewall" Jackson,

(1824–1863) the Confederate hero, was born in Clarksburg, a town that chose to go Union when the Civil War broke out. Jackson's tactical genius and coolness under fire made him the hero of the battles of Bull Run, Antietam and Fredericksburg. He was accidentally shot by his own troops in 1863. Lee called him "irreplaceable."

One of the more interesting things about West Virginia is how many people spend time underneath it. *Most of them are miners, of course, digging out the state's enormous coal reserves, but there are others, too.* **Near the town of White Sulphur Springs, for example, the federal government has hollowed out a huge bunker so the president and congress can go live under West Virginia in case a nuclear attack is ever launched on Washington.**

West Virginia is the most marble-crazy state in the Union. Much of the country's marbles are made here.

New River Gorge
The New River in West Virginia is geologically one of the oldest rivers in the world. It cuts a deep gorge through the state and is crossed by a spectacular steel bridge that, for one day every year, is closed to traffic and opened to bungee freaks and B.A.S.E. jumpers (skydivers who like to skip the airplane part).

West Virginia didn't exist until the Civil War; *it used to be part of Virginia. But when Virginia voted to join the Confederacy, the people in the western part of the state refused to go along. Lincoln recognized them and West Virginia was born.*

WV
VA

Westover
is the hometown of Regina Jennings, who was a custodian at the West Virginia University Law School for over 10 years. When she returned, she donated $93,000, her life savings, to the school for "the kindness I have received from the students and faculty" there. She saved the money, she said, by not living extravagantly and investing income from an inherited rental property. The dean of the school was stunned by the donation and the publicity it generated made Regina a national hero.

HATFIELD AND MCCOY FAMILY REUNION

Matewan. The Hatfields lived (and still live) in West Virginia. The McCoys live across the border in Kentucky. Things are a lot friendlier these days. The annual family reunion photo is so huge they expect it to appear in the Guinness Book of Records someday.

Chuck Yeager,
the ultimate "right stuff" pilot, was the first to go faster than the speed of sound, 662 mph. He did it (with a couple of cracked ribs) on October 14, 1947, in an experimental X-1 jet over the California desert. Yeager is from the town of Myra, WV. (b. 1923)

Hillboro, WV, is the birthplace of Pearl S. Buck who spent 40 years of her life in China (her parents were missionaries). She wrote about those years in her novel *The Good Earth* which was specifically cited by the Nobel Committee when they awarded her the Prize for literature in 1938. First American woman to be so honored.

Nevada is our leading candidate for the **"strange things happen here"** state. For one thing, it's where the U.S. government keeps all our captured aliens (Groom Lake, south-central Nevada, Area 51 — for those who believe). Not too far south of the **aliens** is the Nevada Test Site, an area the size of Rhode Island, where the U.S. government used to detonate A-bombs back in the '50s when we used to do that sort of thing. If you'd like to take a picnic, tourists are allowed in by appointment — bring your Geiger counter. *Meanwhile* in northwestern Nevada, where a rocket-powered car recently set a world record, is the Black Rock Desert. Black Rock Desert is also where the **Burning Man Festival** is held. That's where 10,000 people gather for a few days every Fall, rent 1,200 porta-potties, burn a 40-ft wooden effigy, and do many things both **strange and other.**

GUINNESS
WORLD
RECORD

763.63 MPH

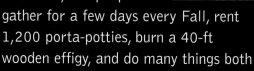

Our Favorite
Spirit Cave Human (d. 7420 B.C.)
The oldest North American mummy was discovered in 1940 during salvage excavations for a guano-mining project. He was found lying on a fur blanket dressed in a skin robe. He wore leather moccasins and had a twined mat sewn around his head and shoulders.

Carson City

Most Famous
Sarah Winnemucca (1842–1891)
Author of Life Among the Paiutes: *Their Wrongs and Claims,* *a history of her tribe. She worked as an interpreter and peacemaker in a U.S. Army camp and a town is named for her.*

Nevada Historical Society.

Las Vegas, the largest city in Nevada, was a town originally founded by Mormon settlers, but it wasn't until the late 1940s when Bugsy Siegel came out from Brooklyn with mob money that he used to build a casino that the modern Las Vegas was launched. Today Las Vegas is home to all ten of the ten biggest hotels in the country, as well as the largest artificial volcano in the world, second largest pyramid, a permanent Canadian circus, two German tiger-loving millionaire magicians, more than 75 full-time Elvis impersonators, and over 1,000 casinos where you can find most anything except clocks. Las Vegas runs on its own unique time.

Nebraska

More than 100 million years ago, Nebraska, the **"Cornhusker State,"** was the bottom of a warm shallow sea (**"the Seafloor State"**). Sixty-three million years later, after things had dried out, wooly mammoths, pre-historic rhinos and bear dogs roamed the state (the world's biggest elephant fossil is **not** from Africa, it's from Nebraska).

Most Famous

Silent film star Harold Lloyd (1893–1950) was born in Burchard, but moved to California to chase the Hollywood dream. The only other silent film comedian to really bear comparison with Chaplin or Keaton.

Valentine ●

Platte River

Omaha ●
★ Lincoln

Our Favorite

Harold Edgerton, "Doc Flash." (1903–1990) The man who perfected high-speed stroboscopic photography while a professor at M.I.T. The milk drop coronet shown here was taken at 1/1,000,000th of a second.

©Harold & Esther Edgerton Foundation, 2000, courtesy of Palm Press, Inc.

These days, one-fourth of Nebraska is covered with rolling hills of sand, and if it weren't for the Oglallah aquifer (an enormous underground "lake") Nebraska might be **better known for camels** than its famous sand hill cranes that stop over in the spring along the muddy Platte River ("too thick to drink, too thin to plow"). ■ More than 40 years ago, the U.S. military dug a huge strategic command center underneath a few acres of hills just south of Omaha. If a nuclear war ever breaks out, some fateful decisions are going to be made by Nebraskans. ■ The original Swanson's TV dinner comes from Omaha (1952). (And what's a TV dinner without a tall glass of **Kool-Aid** from Hastings, NE, to wash it down with?) ■ **Valentine,** 69201. If you send your love letters here first, in a stamped envelope, the post office will postmark it "Valentine, NE" and forward it on your beloved addressee. (Awww...) ■ **Chimney Rock,** a huge stand-alone spire marked the end of the plains for hundreds of immigrant wagon trains. It's a landmark sketched in many 19th-century diaries and journals. ■ A modern manmade version of the same thing? **Carhenge,** a form of Jalopy Art, located near the town of Alliance.

Pikes Peak

The best known mountain in the Colorado Rockies was first spotted by Zebulon Pike in 1806 who immediately declared that the mountain "will never be climbed." Today, a road goes to the top and a race is held on it every year with cars and motorcycles. (Current record for the 12 mile course? A little over ten minutes.) Katharine Lee Bates, a Wellesley professor, was inspired by the view from Pike's Peak to write "America the Beautiful" right there on the top of it.

Jackson County

is where you can find Damifino Mountain. We will go there someday, and when we do, we will make someone ask us where we are. Then we will proudly say...

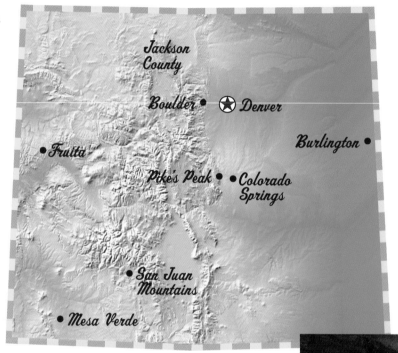

Colorado

Jackson County

Boulder • ☆ Denver

Burlington •

• Fruita

Pike's Peak • Colorado Springs

• San Juan Mountains

• Mesa Verde

Most Famous
Scott Carpenter

(b. 1925) Explorer of outer and undersea space. Carpenter was one of the original Mercury Seven astronauts; he flew the second (nearly ill-fated) American manned orbital flight on May 24, 1962. He later participated in the Navy's Man-in-the-Sea Project as aquanaut in the SEALAB II program off the coast of California.

Mike, the Headless Chicken

Fruita, CO, is where Mike, a chicken, was decapitated by a farmer in 1945. Mike, however, refused to become that night's dinner and lived for another four and a half years. He is to this day celebrated annually in his hometown on "Mike, the Headless Chicken Day." (We are not making this up. Check out: www.h2net.net/p/nslade/mike.html)

ProRodeo Hall of Fame and Museum of the American Cowboy.
The name says it all. Located in Colorado Springs.

Burlington

Kit Carson Carousel, c.1905, nation's oldest wooden carousel.

In1874, a party of 6 trappers decided to forge on through a snowstorm in the San Juan Mountains. When it was over, only one of them walked out,

Alferd Packer

— looking a little too well fed for his own good. After eluding capture for years, Packer was convicted of cannibalism. Legend has it that the judge lectured him sternly: "There were 7 Democrats in the county and you ate 5 of them!" In his honor, the University of Colorado at Boulder's student food court is named The Alferd Packer Grill.

The Denver Mint
produces nearly **20 billion coins** every year (and zero bills). Half of the quarters for the State Quarters program will be stamped with a little "D" right by George's ponytail. And before you even ask, the answer is no, the mint does not have a factory outlet store.

Our Favorite
Lon Cheney

(1883–1930) "The Man of a Thousand Faces." His skills with makeup were legendary. He appeared in many guises in many movies, most famously in The Phantom of the Opera.

Mesa Verde
Tens of thousands of rock and mud dwellings built by the Anasazi who abandoned the area in 1300 AD. Nobody knows why they left.

North Dakota

Most Famous

Most Famous

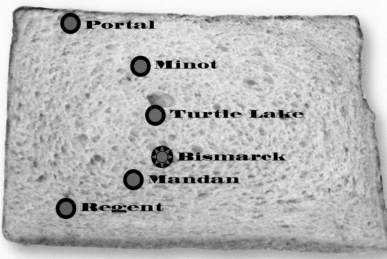

- Portal
- Minot
- Turtle Lake
- Bismarck
- Mandan
- Regent

Our Favorite

Louis L'Amour

(1908–1988) King of the cowboy novel, L'Amour considered himself "just a storyteller, a guy with a seat by the campfire." Before becoming a writer he rode freight trains, worked as an elephant handler and lived with bandits in Tibet.

North Dakota is the most rural of all states — 90% farmland. There are **more** registered **vehicles than people**. *Population in the smallest U.S. town, Hove Mobile Park City, ND — 2. The state is* **number one** *in the U.S. for production of* **wheat**, **barley**, *all types of edible* **beans** *and* **sunflowers**.

Portal

With luck you can shoot an "International Hole in One" at the golf course here. It **straddles** the border with Canada (**the longest unguarded border in the world**).

Turtle Lake

"That one sure can run." Overheard at the Annual **Turtle Racing Championship.**

Bismarck

Capital city. The **tallest** building in the state is here — all **19** stories.

Minot

Annual **combine demolition derby** *at the North Dakota State Fair.*

Phyllis Frelich

(b. 1944) A founding member of the National Theater of the Deaf. Born deaf, she was determined to become an actress despite the initial lack of suitable roles. She's been successful in television and on Broadway.

Mandan

Who says there's not much to do in North Dakota? Rather than just watching the grass grow, attend the **Lawnmower Races** *at the Dacotah Speedway. As they say in Mandan,* "On your mark, get set, **mow**!"

Regent

Sculptor Gary Greff enlisted the help of farmers in the area to construct **giant sculptures** along a desolate stretch of highway in an attempt to attract tourists to the area. Visit the **World's Largest Tin Family** (birds fly in and out of their barbed wire hair), a group of colorful pheasants, Teddy Roosevelt on horseback, or (our favorite) a family of **monster grasshoppers** which stand in a field amidst real identical insects.

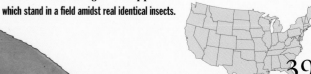

39

Black-footed ferret *lives here; the Most Endangered animal in North America.*

Mount Rushmore
Carved with dynamite and jackhammers, George, Tom, Teddy and Abe's heads are larger than those of the Sphinx and the Statue of Liberty — 60 feet tall. The mountain got its name in 1885 from New York attorney, Charles Rushmore. While riding through the Black Hills he asked the name of the mountain. His guide replied, "Hell, it never had a name, but from now on we'll call the damned thing Rushmore." True story.

Badlands
The middle of nowhere looks like this — steep canyons, jagged rock and miles of desolation. It's eroding at a rate of one inch a year. At this rate, the Badlands will be a flat prairie in a half-million years.

SOUTH DAKOTA

Most Famous
Crazy Horse
(1843–1877)
Oglala Sioux chief known for his tenacious resistance to white expansion into the Native American west. At the Battle of Little Big Horn, he and his warriors killed General Custer and most of his troops. A 563-foot-tall stone monument to Crazy Horse is being carved in the Black Hills near Mount Rushmore. We chose Crazy Horse as "most famous," but Red Cloud and Sitting Bull were also born in South Dakota.

Our Favorite
Myron Floren
(b. 1919) America's most famous accordionist learned to play on a $10 instrument ordered from Sears Roebuck when he was seven.

■ *On August 2, 1876, Jack "Broken Nose" McCall stepped through a saloon door in* **Deadwood** *and shot Wild Bill Hickok from behind. Wild Bill was playing poker at the time, holding* **aces and 8's**. *These days poker players call it "the deadman's hand."*

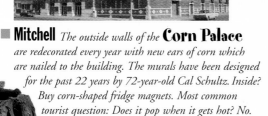

■ **Mitchell** *The outside walls of the* **Corn Palace** *are redecorated every year with new ears of corn which are nailed to the building. The murals have been designed for the past 22 years by 72-year-old Cal Schultz. Inside? Buy corn-shaped fridge magnets. Most common tourist question: Does it pop when it gets hot? No.*

■ **Sturgis**
If you like motorcycles, this is the place to be in August. **The Sturgis Motorcycle Rally** is world famous. Wild Bill Hickok and Calamity Jane are buried here.

☆ **Pierre** If you live here, it's pronounced "peer." State capital.

■ **De Smet** *An annual Laura Ingalls Wilder pageant celebrates the Little House books.*

■ **Sue**, the 41-foot-long (and world's most perfect) *tyrannosaurus rex* skeleton, was discovered near Hill City in 1990. Her head alone weighs 400 pounds. Named after the woman who discovered her, Susan Hendrickson, she was purchased at auction by the Field Museum in Chicago for $8.36 million.

■ **Wall Drug**
It's in the middle of nowhere, but is probably the world's most famous drugstore. Wall Drug got its start during the Depression by offering free ice water to thirsty travelers.

■ **Aberdeen**
L. Frank Baum wrote *The Wizard of Oz* here. Some people think he got the name Oz from his file cabinet drawer...the one labeled O-Z.

Montana

A little more than 800,000 people live in the state of Montana, more or less the same number you'd find in about 34 square miles of New York City. Western Montana is dominated by the Rocky Mountains and Glacier National Park

protects the wildest part of them. It's the greatest park in the lower 48 if you're a grizzly bear. Montana is great dino-digging country. Of the two dozen good specimen T-Rex skeletons ever found anywhere, eight

have been found in Montana. If you'd like to help find the next one, dino-digging summer camps exist for young amateurs: http://labrat3.nmclites. edu/dinosaurs/) *is a possibility. Also* http://www. harleyshirts. com/links/dinosaurs.htm.

Missoula

Hamilton

Mann Gulch

★ Helena

Hamilton
Hollywood goes to Montana. This is where people like Ted Turner and Peter Fonda buy their ranches, in the spectacular Bitterroot Mountains.

Miles City
The self-proclaimed cowboy capital of the world. The Range Riders Museum here has a donut from the Civil War.

Plentywood

Ismay Recently renamed JOE in honor of...guess who?

Miles City

Joe

Litle Big Horn

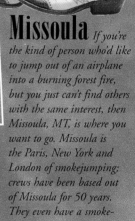

Missoula
If you're the kind of person who'd like to jump out of an airplane into a burning forest fire, but you just can't find others with the same interest, then Missoula, MT, is where you want to go. Missoula is the Paris, New York and London of smokejumping: crews have been based out of Missoula for 50 years. They even have a smoke-jumping museum in town.

Plentywood
Fainting Goats
Almost certainly the most unusual attraction in NE Montana are the fainting goats of sisters Dorothy Brockmier and Linda Halland. The herd suffers from a rare genetic defect which makes them fall over into a faint if they are startled, something that visitors to the farm are eager to do by leaning on the fence and hollering "Hey goat!"

Lewis and Clark

spent a lot of time in Montana looking for a river that ran to the Pacific, the legendary "all-water route." Instead, they found the **Rocky Mountains.** *If you'd like to experience a bit of life as they lived it, we recommend Lolo Hot Springs, near Lolo Pass, where the Corps of Discovery spent a night almost 200 years ago. It's still a great wilderness soak.*

Little Big Horn
This is where Lt. Col. George Armstrong Custer and close to 200 members of the Seventh Cavalry encountered a force of Sioux and Cheyenne Indians led by Crazy Horse and Sitting Bull on June 25, 1876. The battle lasted less than an hour but has reverberated down through the years to become the most famous day in 300 years of hostilities between the Europeans and the native population. Today, the battlefield is a National Monument and yes, re-enactments are staged from time to time.

Mann Gulch
On August 5, 1949, 13 smokejumpers lost their lives here when they were overrun by a fire that "blew up." It was the worst disaster in the history of smokejumping and, about 40 years later, author Norman MacLean immortalized it in his book "Young Men and Fire."

Our Favorite

Jeannette Rankin
(1880–1973) The first female member of the U.S. House of Representatives. Most women in the U.S. couldn't even vote in 1917 when she was first elected.

Most Famous

Charles Russell
(1864–1926) Painter and sculptor of cowboys, Native Americans and all things Western. (Okay, he wasn't actually born in Montana. But he moved there at 16.)

WASHINGTON

SEATTLE

★OLYMPIA

MT. RAINIER

MT. ST. HELENS

Bill Gates

(b.1955) There are hundreds of "wowie zowie" facts about how much money Microsoft co-founder Bill Gates has, but we like this one: Let's say Bill is walking down the street and drops some of his money. Assuming it takes 4 seconds to bend over to pick it back up, how much does it have to be to make it worth his while to stop? $5,000. Anything less than that, keep walking Bill.

Sasquatch

(a.k.a. Bigfoot, Abonimable Snowman, and "Hey, Big Guy in the Gorilla Costume!," b. who knows) *Some people have seen the hairy denizen of the deep woods of Oregon, Washington and Northern California, but it's generally been an "out of the corner of my eye" experience. The fellow reportedly has big feet (duh...) and smells pretty bad. Two guys say they caught a "female" Sasquatch on film in 1967 (looks to us like one of their wives in an ape suit).*

In 1962,

Seattle hosted a world's fair and built its famous Space Needle to loom over the fairgrounds. It's still there, and if you don't mind restaurants that rotate (we do), you can still eat on top of it. Recently, Microsoft billionaire Paul Allen funded the construction of the **Experience Music Project** on the old fairgrounds, a futuristic, high-tech museum **honoring rock and roll.** Personally, we believe Seattle's finest institution is the one and only Archie McPhee store where you can find (among many other things) boxing puppet nuns and glow-in-the-dark rubber jellyfish.

Washington, the only state named after a president, is the smallest state west of the Mississippi (and it's larger than ANY state east of the Mississippi).

SEATTLE
SPACE NEEDLE

Mt. St. Helens

At 8:32 in the morning, on May 18, 1980, Mt. St. Helens erupted with enough force to blow away 4 billion cubic yards of itself, the top 1,000 feet. It was a blast so strong that it stripped trees from hillsides six miles away.

Mt. Rainier

Washington's Mt. Rainier is the most spectacular mountain in the lower 48. *Local Native Americans called it Tahoma, "the source of all waters." Even though it's 84 feet shorter than Mt. Whitney (California) it's a far greater climbing challenge and besides, it's way better looking.*

On November 24, 1971, infamous skyjacker D.B. Cooper jumped out of the back door of a Boeing 727 with $200,000 in ransom cash (he claimed he had a bomb). It was a night jump into freezing rain over Washington wilderness and a lot of people think he died instantly. Of course, a lot of people think he didn't, too. Neither he nor his body have ever been found. (The back doors of all 727's these days have a lock on them that keeps them from being opened mid-flight. It's called the "Cooper vane.")

MOUNT
St. HELENS

OLYMPIC
RAIN FOREST

The Tacoma Narrows Bridge disaster

On November 7, 1940, during a severe wind storm, the bridge across the Tacoma Narrows began to vibrate like a guitar string. In some of the most famous disaster footage ever shot, a local man captured the moment as the bridge shook itself apart. It had only been open to traffic for four months.

APPLES
CHERRIES & HOPS

Washington is known for apples, cherries and hops. The hops, a key ingredient in beer, may account for some of the Sasquatch sightings in the state. By the way, why does Bigfoot paint his toenails red? So he can hide in apple and cherry trees. Ever seen Bigfoot? Works pretty well doesn't it?

D.B. COOPER

If you're ready for big time boardsailing, you'll need to go to "the gorge" — Washington's Columbia River gorge — where the **serious board-heads** hang out. At various points in the gorge, the wind can easily range from 15 to 35 mph.

Idaho

Most Famous
Picabo Street

(b. 1971) Fast skier. She joined the U.S. Ski Team in 1989 when she was 17. Seven years later, she became the only American skier to ever win a World Cup downhill championship. Picabo is named after the Idaho town of — what else — Picabo.

Idaho is the only state in the Union never to have been owned by a foreign nation. It is dominated by its mountains and roadless wilderness. (If the state were ironed out, it would probably be bigger than Texas.)

① Lake Pend Oreille

At 1,158 feet deep, it's a Navy testing lake for submarines.

Potatoes

Boise's airport is one of the very few where you can find vending machines serving French fries (not that bad, actually). Idaho is the country's leading grower of potatoes and supplies McDonald's with most of its fries.

Owyhee County

in the southwest corner of the state, was named in honor of Hawaii (by locals unburdened by the rules of ordinary spelling).

② Arco
Site of the first nuclear-powered electricity in the U.S.

③ Yellow Pine

Our favorite little mountain town in the west. One main street (dirt) with a couple of sleeping dogs in the middle of it.

Ernest Hemingway's final resting place

Hemingway was an Idaho kind of guy who spent his last years at a cabin near Sun Valley. The fly fishing and hunting suited him.

Ezra Pound
Idaho's least likely native son. Born in Hailey. One of the 20th century's more controversial intellectuals. Pound was a renowned poet, literary critic, writer — and, during World War II (which he spent in Italy), a public supporter of the dictator Mussolini. Afterwards, he was returned to the U.S. and convicted of treason. He spent his last years in a mental health facility.

Boise
32% of the state's population lives in the capital area. (Current most amazing Idaho fact? The entire state is still a single area code.)

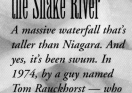

Shoshone Falls on the Snake River

A massive waterfall that's taller than Niagara. And yes, it's been swum. In 1974, by a guy named Tom Rauckhorst — who lived to tell the tale.

④ Twin Falls

Professional crazy guy Evel Knievel tried to jump the 1,600-foot-wide Snake River gorge in his rocket-powered Sky Cycle X-3 in 1974. Didn't quite make it. His parachute opened too soon, but he survived the 470 ft fall.

⑤ The Frank Church River of No Return Wilderness Area

The largest wilderness area in the lower 48.

Our Favorite
Gutzon Borglum

(1856–1941) Sculptor with a big idea — Mount Rushmore. He was also the first sculptor to attempt to carve a Confederate memorial on Stone Mountain in Georgia.

⑥ Sun Valley

Ever since Clark Gable and his pals started coming here in the '30s, Sun Valley has been one of the West's glitziest resorts. If you're arriving by private jet, get in line, parking's tight in peak season.(P.S. Like most people, you've probably wondered where the Hokey Pokey and Bunny Hop were invented. *Answer: Sun Valley.*)

Jackson Pollock

(1912–1956) Painter of "I could-have-painted-that" splattery paintings. However, he invented the technique of applying paint by dipping and flinging it against canvas and we didn't.

Yellowstone

National Park. One of the modern wonders of the world. *The nation's oldest national park sits on top of a "hot spot," a place where the planet's red-hot core reaches a little closer to the surface. Result? A whole lot of spouting geysers and hot springs.*

Wyoming has a head-count under 500,000, fewest in the nation.

Towns are so scattered that Wyomingites don't think twice about a 100-mile jaunt. After all, they live in a state where traffic jams and rush hours are only on TV. Of course, the open road has a price. *Driving is far more dangerous in Wyoming than New York or California, thanks to all of* the state's long and lonely 2-lane highways.

W*Y*O*M*I*N*G

(Connect the horseshoes and you have Wyoming.)

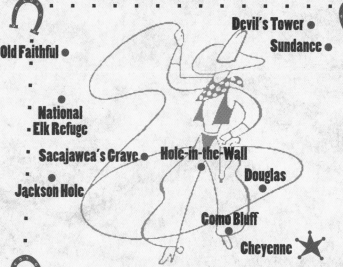

Old Faithful •

Devil's Tower •

Sundance •

• National Elk Refuge

• Sacajawea's Grave

Hole-in-the-Wall

Douglas

Jackson Hole

Como Bluff

Cheyenne ★

Women's Rights

In 1869, before it was a state, Wyoming passed a law giving women the right to vote. At the time, no state in the union permitted such an incredible thing. In fact, 11 years later, the U.S. Congress threatened to withhold statehood unless Wyomingites revoked the law. No dice.

Hole-in-the-Wall

A famed outlaw hangout of the 19th century. Butch Cassidy and the Sundance Kid (their mothers knew them as Robert Leroy Parker and Harry Longabaugh) used to hide out around here.

The Grand Tetons

One of the country's premier climbing areas. Epic tales of disasters, both near and otherwise, are told by climbers of the Tetons and the nearby Wind Rivers.

Rulon Gardner

(b. 1971) The 2000 Olympic gold-medal winner for super heavyweight wrestling grew up on a farm in Wyoming, the youngest of nine children. He defeated Russian Alexander Karelin who had not lost a match in 10 years.

Jackalopes

Douglas, WY, is the Jackalope capital of the universe. A local taxidermist first showed one off in 1934.

Devil's Tower

An 800-foot sheer-sided vertical stick of cooled lava in N.E. Wyoming that looks like clear evidence of ancient aliens to us. In 1941, a stunt parachutist landed on top of it and forced a nationwide scramble to find climbers skilled enough to get him down.

Como Bluff

It seems clear from the evidence that Wyoming was once a very popular state with the dinosaurs. Based on the number of fossils already found there, one site, the world-famous Como Bluff, must have been a dinosaur Times Square.

Jackson Hole

The Aspen of Wyoming. Might be the only town in the state where you can get designer underwear.

UTAH

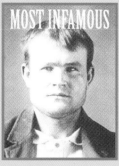

Butch Cassidy
1866–1909

Train robber, bank robber, leader of the Hole-in-the-Wall Gang.

Promontory Summit, UT,

is where you can find a historic site marking **the exact spot** where the first transcontinental railroad was officially finished with the driving of a golden spike. **Except it wasn't.** The real place is in Strasburg, CO.

☆ Salt Lake City

Founded by Mormon leader Brigham Young and his band of religious refugees in 1847, it is best known today as the town where **Juggling For the Complete Klutz** *has been printed for 20 years (over 2 1/2 million copies). Also, in much the same vein, it's the nation's leading center of* rubber chicken *manufacturing.*

OUR FAVORITE

Philo T. Farnsworth 1906–1971
Inventor of TV

A Mormon farm boy by the name of Philo T. Farnsworth dreamt up the idea of an electronic machine that could send pictures through the air when he was only 15 years old. Six years later, in 1927, he built a prototype that proved he wasn't crazy.

Bonneville Salt Flats.
Nine miles of dead flat without a speed limit in sight. If your car has a speedometer that goes up to 600 mph, this is where you want to be.

The Great Salt Lake

One of the world's harder lakes to drown in. **BIG, WARM, AND KIND OF YUCKY.** *Almost salty enough to float a brick in.*

Cottonwood Canyon

Curious about your ancestors? Hollowed into a **bombproof mountain** *near Salt Lake City is the planet's* largest library of birth, death and marriage records. *Chances are, they have your name.*

MOAB *When mountain bikers die and go to heaven, they end up in Moab,* **a town where the bike shops outnumber the grocery stores, seven to one.**

Down Winders

During the 1950s, the U.S. government exploded atomic bombs *on the Nevada test range upwind of southern Utah. In the years since, the ranchers and townsfolk who lived there at the time have come to call themselves "downwinders."*

Bryce Canyon
National Park
Slot canyons, flash floods, weird weather, desert whirlwinds and **hoodoo** *rock formations…it's all right here. As a former Bryce Canyon rancher described it,* "**a heckuva a place to lose a cow.**"

Canyonlands
National Park.
Over the past 10 million years, Canyonlands has been cut, carved, chopped, sliced and diced by the Green and Colorado rivers.

Arches National Park
Rocks that are carved by wind and sand into natural bridges are geologic bubbles *– here today, gone in a mere 500,000 years. Right here is where you can catch a bunch of them today.*

Zion National Park

Big Rock Candy Mountain
This caramel-colored formation of decomposed volcanic rock was **made famous by the song** of the same name.

Park City
Sundance Film Festival

They've got a lot of them, but **tumbleweeds** aren't native to Utah. They're invaders from Russia, brought here accidentally by Ukrainian farmers who were trying to grow flax.

45

Oklahoma

The town of Boise City, OK, was bombed in World War II. By the U.S. Naval Air Corps. By mistake.

The town of Beaver sponsors the annual **World Championship Cow Chip Throw.** The current record (set in 1979) is 182.3 feet.

MOST FAMOUS
Will Rogers (1879–1935)

The country's best-loved folk-philosopher and political writer during the '20s and '30s. Started out as a joke-telling cowboy, died (in an Alaska plane crash) a national treasure. Quote: "I never met a man I didn't like."

• Boise City   • Beaver

CHISHOLM TRAIL

ROUTE 66

Woody Guthrie, the well-known folksinger from Okemah, OK, *sang about the "Okies" in some of his best-known songs.*

The **Oklahoma Oil Boom** *started in Bartlesville, OK, in 1897 and created its own kind of greasy Gold Rush. Before 1940, oil had been discovered under more than half the counties in Oklahoma (there's an oil rig sitting in front of the state capital building today).*

The Chisholm Trail, used by cowboys to drive cattle from Texas to markets in the North. Millions of cattle walked this route. Cowboys were paid by the month; cooks got paid more, cows got...well, you know...

Route 66 — famous for motels, tacky signs, gas stations, free spirits and your kicks — *cuts straight through Oklahoma. Farmers driven out of Oklahoma by the dust storms of 1933 used it to travel to the "golden fields of California." Read Steinbeck's* Grapes of Wrath *for the best Route 66 story.*

OUR FAVORITE
Martin Gardner (b. 1914)

"One of the great intellects in recent times," Martin Gardner has published over 100 books on math, philosophy, magic, frauds and quackery, the theory of relativity, games, Lewis Carroll, the Wizard of Oz, Casey at the Bat and other topics.

Oklahoma City *is the state capital and was the* **birthplace of both the shopping cart (1937)** *and the* **parking meter (1935).**

At one time, Oklahoma was completely and legally owned by Native Americans, making it officially off-limits to settlers. *That ended at the stroke of noon, April 22, 1889, the hour that President Harrison announced would be the Grand Opening of the Indian Territory to anyone who could get in there and stake a claim to 160 acres — first come first served. Thousands took him up and tore across the state. Oklahoma City went from near nothing to 25,000 population in 24 hours. Cheaters who sneaked in ahead of the gun were called "Sooners."*

New Mexico

Gallup, the largest Native American town in the U.S., where pickup trucks outnumber cars 2:1.

Albuquerque, home to a huge hot air balloon festival (never mind the International Rattlesnake Museum).

Roswell, NM.

The Official UFO Capital of the United States of America. On June 14, 1947, large chunks of mysterious junk led base commanders at Roswell Army Air Field to issue the following statement (retracted the next day): "We have in our possession a flying saucer." A 1997 governmental report stated it was "remains of an experimental weather balloon."

Yeah, right.

At the Star Child gift shop in Roswell you can buy a T-shirt that says: "I was abducted by aliens and all I got was this stupid T-shirt."

Most Famous

First pictured on a fire prevention poster in 1944, a real live Smokey was found after a forest fire near Capitan, New Mexico, in 1950. Official name: Smokey Bear (no middle name). Official song: "Smokey the Bear."

Check out **Toilet rock** in the City of Rocks State Park. Looks like the real thing.

Truth or Consequences used to be Hot Springs, NM, but they changed the name in 1950 in exchange for prizes and publicity from the producers of the hit radio show Truth or Consequences. Locals call the place "T or C."

CHACO CANYON is typical. Anasazi ("the ancient ones") occupied this area from circa 1000 AD to 1200 AD. Then vanished. They built stone pueblos in cliffs that look a lot like modern apartments ("Hi, I'm in pueblo 3-C…."). They were good calendar people too.

(map labels) Gallup · SANTE FE · ALBUQUERQUE · TRINITY SITE · TRUTH OR CONSEQUENCES · ROSWELL · COLUMBUS

COLUMBUS In 1923 Pancho Villa crossed the border here with 1,500 semi-regular Mexican Soldiers. It was the only foreign invasion of the United States in the twentieth century.

TRINITY SITE.

July 16, 1945, at the White Sands missile range, near Alamogordo, NM, the first man-made nuclear explosion went off. Visitors are allowed there for 90 minutes only on the first Saturday in October. No food allowed.

CARLSBAD TAVERNS have millions of bats (but there are no major league baseball teams in NM). It is a huge cave room big enough to hold 14 football games simultaneously.

Our Favorite

Maria Martinez (1887–1980) Pueblo artist famous for her black-on-black pottery.

ARIZONA

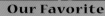

Most Famous

Geronimo
(1829–1909)

Chiricahua Apache war chief and a fearless renegade. His name was immortalized by American parachute troops who made it their official leaving-the-airplane holler.

Grand Canyon

The planet's most amazing crack in the ground. In 2 billion years, the Colorado River has done some serious rock carving. Our advice? If you only have time to do one thing in this life, make it a visit to the Grand Canyon.

Oraibi

This Hopi town, still populated, is the oldest town in the U.S. (1500 years older than New York).

Chandler

In March, jockeys ride ostriches as if they were thoroughbreds at the Chandler Ostrich Festival.

Our Favorite

Cesar Chavez
(1927–1993)

The son of illegal immigrants, Cesar Chavez spent his childhood as a fieldworker in Arizona. It was an experience that led him to a lifetime of labor organization and the creation of the United Farmworkers Association.

KTNN

A radio station that broadcasts exclusively in the Navajo language. 660 on your AM radio dial whenever you're in the Four Corners area.

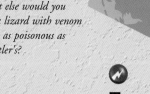

Gila Monster

What else would you call a lizard with venom twice as poisonous as a rattler's?

Meteor Crater

50,000 years ago, a very, very big rock from outer space hit right here creating one of the best-looking craters on the planet.

Flagstaff

The first person ever to see the planet Pluto, Clyde Tombaugh in 1930, was here at the Lowell Observatory. Arizona is the best state in the lower 48 for astronomers and their telescopes.

Cochise's Stronghold

Hiding place of the great Apache chief Cochise.

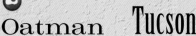

Oatman

Every 4th of July, folks in Oatman do what other people in hot towns only talk about: They fry eggs on the sidewalks.

Tucson

Might be the best summer lightning town in the country.

Saguaro Cactus

Big saguaros are old (100+ years), prickly and valuable. Cactus rustlers will dig one up and sell it for thousands. Cactus cops roam the desert to stop them. ("Put that cactus down, back away slowly and nobody gets hurt.")

Phoenix

Ruby the talented elephant used to be from Phoenix. She lived in the zoo and painted in watercolor and oils. (Don't laugh. They sold for hundreds of dollars apiece.)

Navajo Code Talkers

During WWII, Navajos were recruited as battlefield radio operators to speak in their native tongue, an instant uncrackable military code.

Superstition Mountains

"The Lost Dutchman Gold Mine" is up here somewhere, a fortune just waiting for you. Or not.

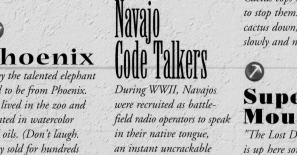

48

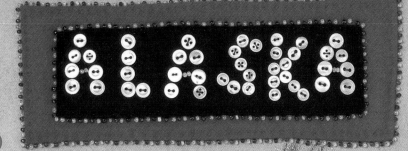

Most Famous

Balto

In 1925, Balto (d. 1933), a sled dog, led a dogsled team 660 miles through a blizzard from Anchorage to Nome to deliver medicine for a potentially deadly diphtheria epidemic. Today's Iditerod follows Balto's route.

Fairbanks, *is plenty cold (-4 degrees below is the average high in winter), but it is such a dry town that it gets less snowfall than Salt Lake City, Utah.*

There are more **eagles** and **grizzlies** *in Alaska than all the other states combined. Alaska also leads the nation in* **outhouses,** *oil production, and unmarried men. These facts might be connected.*

The McDonald's on Northern Lights Blvd. in **Anchorage,** *AK, is among the* **top seven** *most profitable in the U.S. (Big Macs go for $2.79).*

Our Favorite

Benny Benson

Benny Benson (1913–1972) designed the Alaska flag in 1926 when he was 13. His design was the winner in a territorial flag contest; he won $1,000 and a gold watch engraved with the flag.

Approximately **1** out of every **50** Alaskans flies his or her own airplane.

People who say the Alaskan state bird is the **mosquito** and its state flower the **55-gallon drum** are not telling the truth.

Matanuska Valley, *in southern Alaska, grows* **cabbages** *and* **lettuce** *of Guinness World Record size.*

Alentian Islands

Alaska has a population of about **700,000** people (about half what it has in caribou). Interesting comparison: If you traveled a route from Chicago to New York in 1776, it would be about as long and as crowded as a trip from Anchorage to Pt. Barrow is today.

Alaska was actually **purchased** *from Russia in 1867 for about $7,000,000. Nice price. At that rate the planet would cost $2.5 billion and Bill Gates could* **buy the whole thing** *(and realize his ultimate dream?).*

The **only** *time U.S. soil was actually invaded during WWII was on* **Dutch Harbor,** *an Aleutian Island, by a* **Japanese** *force.*

Mt. McKinley, *known by its native name Denali, is the highest point in North America. More than 1,000 people try to climb it every year. Only about 600 actually make it all the way.*

Juneau, the state capital (accessible by boat and airplane only)

The Alaskan fact most likely to win you a **trivia contest:** *The chain of Aleutian Islands* **crosses** *the International Dateline making the state of Alaska (technically) farther* **East** *AND farther* **West** *than any other. Weirdest statistic: About* **one** *out of every eleven Alaskans has been in a* **moose or caribou wreck.**

Little Diomede Island *in the Bering Straits has a nice view of* **Russia** *(making Russia our closest neighbor if you exclude Mexico and Canada).*

HAWAII

Honolulu

FEET

15,000

10,000

5,000

0

5,000

10,000

15,000

The **tallest** mountain on Earth (if you ignore the water) is **Mauna Kea** which dominates the big island of Hawaii. It's 2,965 feet taller than **Mt. Everest**, measured from the seafloor. The upper slopes of the mountain get enough snow to make **skiing** possible. The summit itself has got the **highest concentration of telescopes** (and astronomy PhDs) in the country since the night skies are **clearer** here than anywhere else on Earth.

OUR FAVORITE

Salevaa Fuauli Atisanoe (a.k.a. Konishiki, b. 1967) Awesome sumo wrestler (retired) and rap artist. He's said to rank with Hello Kitty, Mickey Mouse and Ultraman in popularity with Japanese children.

MOST FAMOUS

Duke Paoa Kahanamoku (1890–1968) "The Father of Modern Surfing," Kahanamoku also won three Olympic gold medals for swimming. Quote: "Out of water I am nothing."

Mt. Everest
29,035 ft.

50

ACKNOWLEDGMENTS

Stateswoman:
Marilyn Green (born in Michigan)

Quarterback:
John Cassidy (New Jersey)

Designers:
Sandra McHenry (Montana) and Hilary Davis (Connecticut)/Sandra McHenry Design; Maria Seamans (California)

Art Director:
MaryEllen Podgorski (Connecticut)

Art Editor:
Marta Kongsle (Oklahoma)

Photo Research:
Stephen Forsling, Susan Friedman

Researchers:
Jan Adkins, Kevin Altamirano, Erin Barrett, Rebecca Center, Pallen Chiu, Bob Fenster, Elizabeth Khoo, Jack Mingo, Beth Perrine, Marcia Vastine, Courtney Yin, Sara Zarr

Folio Maps:
Eureka Cartography

Illustration: Johnny Karwan. St. Louis arch, frog: Digital Imagery© copyright 2000 PhotoDisc, Inc. 7-Up can: Tom Upton. Pony Express: Dover Publications. **Page 25, Arkansas:** Map cookie: Jennifer Presley. Bill Clinton, Dizzy Dean: © Bettmann/CORBIS. Fishing lures: Radlund & Associates/Artville. Illustrations: Elwood H. Smith. **Page 26, Michigan:** Map, title: Eureka Cartography/David Barker. Henry Ford, Magic Johnson: © Bettmann/CORBIS. Kellogg's® Frosted Flakes®, Kellogg's Froot Loops® and Kellogg's Smacks® are registered trademarks of Kellogg Company. All rights reserved. Used with permission. Bread slicer: Oliver Products, Inc. Cat: Digital Imagery© copyright 2000 PhotoDisc, Inc. Plate: Tom Upton. **Page 27, Florida:** Map: David Barker. Jim Morrison: © The Memory Shop/Sygma. Manatee: © Brandon D. Cole/ CORBIS. Gators: Courtesy Gatorland, Orlando, FL. Turtle: Melanie Marder Parks. Space shuttle: Digital Imagery© copyright 2000 PhotoDisc, Inc. Certificate: Maria Seamans. Dancers on beach: © Bettmann/CORBIS. Clown shoes: Digital Imagery© copyright 2000 PhotoDisc, Inc. Orange: Artville. Football player: Jock McDonald. This copy of the National Enquirer was read from cover to cover. **Page 28, Texas:** Map, soda can: Tom Upton. Red Adair: © Paul Howell/Gamma-Liaison. Sandra Day O'Connor: © Roger Ressmeyer/CORBIS. Barney: © Reuters NewMedia Inc./CORBIS. Cowgirls: © Bettmann/ CORBIS. Cadillac Ranch sign: © Joseph Sohm; Chromosohm Inc./CORBIS. Alamo: Digital Imagery© copyright 2000 PhotoDisc, Inc. Baseball: Radlund & Associates/Artville. Cockroach: © Robert & Linda Mitchell. "Cowasaki" art car: Harrod Blank/Larry Fuente. Bat: Daniela Perani. **Page 29, Iowa:** Map: David Barker. Grant Wood: Grant Wood, Self-Portrait, 1932. Oil on masonite panel. Collection of Davenport Museum of Art. Museum purchase, Acquisition Fund 65.1. © Estate of Grant Wood/Licensed by VAGA, New York, N.Y. Corn holders: Joseph Quever. Illustrations: Elwood H. Smith. American Gothic kids: Peter Fox. **Page 30, Wisconsin:** Map: David Barker. Harry Houdini, Georgia O'Keeffe: © CORBIS. Motorcycle: Courtesy Harley-Davidson Motor Company. Hall of Fame: Courtesy Freshwater Fishing Hall of Fame. Bratwurst trophy: © John Brozovich. Yo-yo: Peter Fox. **Page 31, California:** Maps: David Barker. Amy Tan: © Gregory Pace/Sygma. Jack London: © Bettmann/ CORBIS. **Page 32, Minnesota:** Illustrations: Robert Zimmerman (no relation). **Page 33, Oregon:** Map: David Barker. Rose pin: Tom Upton. Matt Groening: © R. Melloul/Sygma. Beverly Cleary: Courtesy HarperCollins Publishers. Bear, Crater

Lake, rubber duck: Digital Imagery© copyright 2000 PhotoDisc, Inc. Bozo: © Kevin Fleming/ CORBIS. Keiko: © Thomas Jouanneau/Sygma. Umbrella: Peter Fox. Harvey County Sagebrush Orchestra of 1915: Oregon Historical Society, negative number 14287. **Page 34, Kansas:** Illustration: Buc Rogers. Buster Keaton: © Hulton-Deutsch Collection/CORBIS. Amelia Earhart: © Bettmann/CORBIS. **Page 35, West Virginia:** Marbles: Joseph Quever. Loose marbles: Digital Imagery© copyright 2000 PhotoDisc, Inc. Stonewall Jackson: © The Corcoran Gallery of Art/CORBIS. Chuck Yeager, coal miners: © Bettmann/CORBIS. Hatfield clan: © Bettmann/ CORBIS. Jumping: © Whitewater Photography. Piggy bank: Digital imagery© copyright 2000 PhotoDisc, Inc. WV/VA map: Eureka Cartography. **Page 36, Nevada:** Map, title: David Barker. Sarah Winnemucca Nevada Historical Society. Spirit Cave Human: Courtesy Nevada State Museum and the Fallon-Paiute Shoshone Tribe. Thrust SSC: © Peter Brock/Liaison. Wedding chapel: © Dave Bartruff/ CORBIS. Burning Man by Larry Harvey and Jerry James; photograph by William Binzen. Elvis cards from King's Kards © Patty Carroll. Alien: from Invasion of the Saucerman. **Page 37, Nebraska:** Illustration: Daniela Perani. Harold Lloyd: © Harold Lloyd Estate. Reprinted with permission. Courtesy of the Academy of Motion Picture Arts and Sciences. Photograph by Dr. Harold E. Edgerton. ©Harold & Esther Edgerton Foundation, 2000, courtesy of Palm Press, Inc. **Page 38, Colorado:** Map: Eureka Cartography. Lon Chaney (as in Phantom of the Opera): Kobal Collection; (as himself): Photofest. Scott Carpenter: NASA. Carousel: Courtesy Kit Carson County Carousel Association. Mesa Verde: Digital Imagery© copyright 2000 PhotoDisc, Inc. Quarter: Tom Upton. **Page 39, North Dakota:** Map: David Barker. Louis L'Amour: © Roger Ressmeyer/CORBIS. Phyllis Frelich: © AP Wide World Photos. Grain elevator: © Vince Streano/CORBIS. Lawn mower races: © Will Kincaid. Giant grasshopper: Drew McCalley. Golfing dog: Ed Taber. Boy with turtle: Peter Fox. **Page 40, South Dakota:** Map: outline, Eureka Cartography; Mt. Rushmore, Digital Imagery© copyright 2000 PhotoDisc, Inc. Myron Floren: Courtesy of the South Dakota State Historical Society. Crazy Horse: © Bettmann/CORBIS. Black-footed ferret: © Jeff Vanuga/CORBIS. Crazy Horse Memorial: © Buddy Mays/CORBIS. Sue T. Rex: © Reuters/M.P. Weinstein/Archive Photos. Wall Drug: © Paul Horsted/Dakota Photographic LLC. Working on Mt. Rushmore: © Underwood & Underwood/CORBIS. Motorcycle: Courtesy Harley-Davidson Motor Company. Corn Palace: Digital Imagery© copyright

2000 PhotoDisc, Inc. **Page 41, Montana:** Outline map: Eureka Cartography. Charles Russell: Montana Historical Society. Jeanette Rankin: © CORBIS. Lewis & Clark drawing: From the Lewis and Clark Journals (917.3 L58 Codex J:80). Courtesy American Philosophical Society. Grizzly bear, cowboy boots, Glacier National Park: Digital Imagery© copyright 2000 PhotoDisc, Inc. T. Rex: photograph by Greg Epperson. **Page 42, Washington:** Illustrations: Laura Smith. Bill Gates: © Reuters NewMedia Inc./CORBIS. Sasquatch: Digital Imagery© copyright 2000 PhotoDisc, Inc. **Page 43, Idaho:** Map and title: Bob Esparza. Ketchup bottle: Joseph Quever. Gutzon Borglum: © Underwood & Underwood/CORBIS. Picabo Street: © Stefano Rellandrini/AP Wide World Photos. Shoshone Falls: © David Muench/CORBIS. Evel Knievel: AP Photofile. Clark Gable skiing: © Bettmann/CORBIS. **Page 44, Wyoming:** Jackson Pollock: © Rudolph Burckhardt/Sygma. Old Faithful, Devil's Tower, open range: Digital Imagery© copyright 2000 PhotoDisc, Inc. Rulon Gardner: © Reuters NewMedia Inc/CORBIS. Kid photos, dinosaur: Peter Fox. **Page 45, Utah:** Map: Jim Dryden. Butch Cassidy: © Jonathan Blair/CORBIS. Philo T. Farnsworth: © Bettmann/CORBIS. Juggling book: Peter Fox. **Page 46, Oklahoma:** Illustration: Mark Stutzman. **Page 47, New Mexico:** Illustration: Paine Proffitt. Smokey the Bear: Courtesy Smokey Bear Historical State Park. Maria Martinez: © Horace Bristol/CORBIS. Chaco Canyon: © David Muench/CORBIS. Skull: Artville. **Page 48, Arizona:** Illustration: Nancy Stahl. **Page 49, Alaska:** Map needlework by Marilyn Green; photograph by Joseph Quever. Balto: © Bettmann/CORBIS. Benny Benson: Alaska State Library, Photo No. PCA 01-1921. Eagle, Mt. McKinley/Denali: Digital Imagery© copyright 2000 PhotoDisc, Inc. Giant cabbage: © 2000 John V. R. Evans. **Page 50, Hawaii:** Map: Eureka Cartography. Illustration and frames: Franco Tempesta. Konishiki: © Vandystadt/Allsport USA. Duke: © Hulton-Deutsch Collection/CORBIS. **Pages 51, 52:** State cookies made by Marilyn Green, photographed by Tom Upton. **Page 53:** Kid photos: Peter Fox **Page 54:** Kid photos: Peter Fox **Page 55:** Coins: Tom Upton. **Back Cover:** Map: John & Wendy Illustration. **Models:** Veronica Woodward, Jill Turney, Josh Schneck, Elizabeth Reni-Podgorski, Elliott Perlmutter, Chiara Leifer, Rick Marino, Georgia Rae Herzog, Kayla Fox, Jenner Fox, DeWitt Durham, Max DeLance, Gaby Cahill.

We hope you enjoyed reading The Completely Amazing Slightly Outrageous State Quarters Atlas and Album as much as we enjoyed writing it!

If you'd like to get The Klutz Catalog, just answer this lengthy questionnaire. Grab the nearest pen, fill in the blanks, throw on some postage, and send it our way. Check out every dang thing we do (and activities, too) on our website: klutz.com

CUT IT OUT!

Fill it in, add a stamp, mail, wait impatiently...

Klutz Catalog!

You can order the entire library of 100% Klutz certified books and a diverse collection of other things we happen to like from The Klutz Catalog. It is, in all modesty, unlike any other catalog — and it's yours for the asking.

Who are you?

Name: _____ Age: _____ ❑ Too high to count ○ Boy ○ Girl

Address: _____

City: _____ State: _____ Zip: _____

My Bright Ideas!

Tell us what you think of this book: _____

_____

What would you like us to write a book about? _____

_____

❑ Check this box if you want us to send you The Klutz Catalog.

If you're a grown-up who'd like to hear about new Klutz stuff, give us your e-mail address and we'll stay in touch.

E-mail address: _____

State Quarters